Cortland W. Warrington

DELAWARE'S COASTAL DEFENSES

FORT SAULSBURY
&
A MIGHTY FORT CALLED MILES

by

C.W. Warrington

Reprinted by
Delaware Heritage Press, 2003

DELAWARE'S COASTAL DEFENSES

FORT SAULSBURY
&
A MIGHTY FORT CALLED MILES

by C.W. Warrington

Copyright © 2003
Delaware Heritage Press

A Delaware Heritage Press Book

First printing *A Mighty Fort Called Miles,* 1972
First printing *Fort Saulsbury*, 1991

ISBN: 0-924117-26-5

Library of Congress Control Number: 2003107362

Delaware Heritage Commission
Carvel State Office Building
820 N. French St, 4th Floor
Wilmington, DE 19801

CONTENTS

The Delaware Heritage Commission would like to thank
Leland Jennings from the Cultural Resources and
Recreational Services Section of the Delaware
Department of Parks and Recreation for his assistance in
the preparation of this reprint.

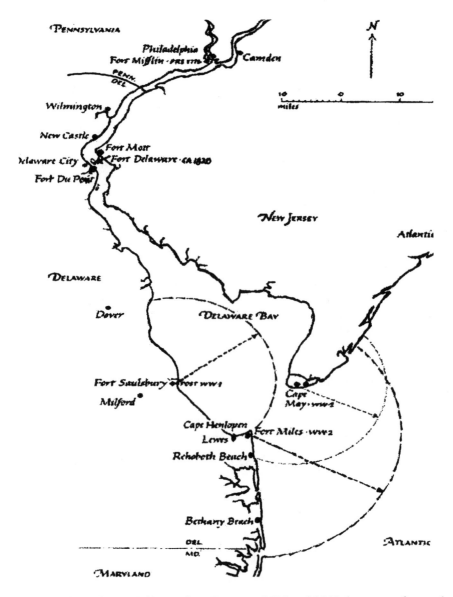

Map of the Delaware River region. Between 1800 and 1945 the range of coastal artillery advanced by a factor of 25. This meant wider channels could be defended and that the water area covered from shore artillery (as shown by arcs) increased more than six hundred times.

(Map from *Seacoast Fortifications of the United States*
Smithsonian Institute Press, 1970.)

iv

HISTORICAL PERSPECTIVE

In order to better enjoy the stories of Fort Miles and Saulsbury written by C.W. Warrington (which follow), the Delaware Heritage Commission believes it useful to include a brief history of coastal defense in our area. The following history has been developed for the Delaware Division of Parks by Elizabeth Ross.

OVERVIEW

Although American seacoast defense systems span one hundred and fifty years and are typically broken into eight separate chronological orders beginning with the First System (1794-1800), a comprehensive federally funded policy of protecting the American coastline did not begin until after the War of 1812. This federal policy of coastal defense, known as the "Third System," "promoted the construction of a chain of fortresses along the American coast from 1820 through the 1950s." Third System fortifications played a significant role in harbor defenses through the Civil War. Built in the early nineteenth century on Pea Patch Island in the Delaware River, Fort Delaware was one of these strategically located fortresses. The protection of the nation's harbors and coasts would remain a vital undertaking of the federal government and continue along coastal waterways well into the mid-twentieth century as new methods in fortification arose to defend against and implement improved armament technologies. Fort Delaware was followed by an Endicott Period fortification, Fort DuPont (1900) and the Post-World War I fortification Fort Saulsbury (1918), each built further south along the Delaware River, each providing a defense farther away from strategic ports and harbors. Technological improvements in fort construction and armament enabled this southward movement and ultimately culminated in the WWII installation at the mouth of the Delaware Bay. By 1941, Fort Miles replaced Fort DuPont as the principal fortification along the Delaware River and Bay. Furthermore, Fort Miles not only represents the zenith of a one hundred and fifty year-long federal coastal defense strategy, but also stands as the last example of the national coastal defense program. By 1950, through the advent of carrier-borne air attack and intercontinental ballistic missiles, coastal defense systems ceased to provide adequate defense of the nation's borders. Therefore, Fort Miles reflects not only a brief period of military history, but also represents the culmination of Seacoast defense strategy and technology and is the last fortification along the Delaware to be built in accordance with such military strategy.

FORT MILES AND FEDERAL COAST DEFENSE STRATEGY, 1800-1945

As a maritime nation with extensive shorelines, the United States relied on its Navy for its first line of defense and upon a system of coastal fortifications for its second line of defense from the 1790s through the 1940s. With 150 years, eight categorical generations of coastal defenses appeared on the American Military Landscape. Fort Miles, commissioned in 1941, represented the last generation of coastal fortifications, known as WWII Forts. By WWII, eighteen harbor defense commands through the U.S. protected America's coastlines, among them, the Harbor Defenses of the Delaware. Replacing Fort DuPont as the headquarters of the Harbor Defenses of the Delaware, Fort Miles provided the first line of defense for the Delaware River and Bay from 1941 through 1945. Its charge was the protection of the Delaware Estuary—the gateway to important industrial, military, and commercial centers such as Wilmington, Trenton, Camden and Philadelphia. The building of Fort Miles symbolized the pinnacle in a century and a half-long coastal defense policy that saw the construction and demolition of numerous posts along the Delaware River.

Gun battery at Fort Miles as it appeared in 1973.
Note that the large opening for the 16-inch gun has been sealed by
a block wall with a steel door in the center.
(Courtesy of C.W. Warrington)

THE PERMANENT SYSTEM

The British invasion during the War of 1812 heightened Americans' fear of a war fought on home soil, and demonstrated the inadequacy of earlier systems of defense. In the wake of the war, the United States government developed a policy of Coastal Defense known as the "Permanent System of National Defense" or "Third System." Sea power represented the major instrument of war against the United States in the early nineteenth century as well as the country's primary defense. Therefore, the masonry fortifications constructed under the new policy were positioned to meet several goals. One set of fortresses denied a foreign fleet access to naval depots, harbors of rendezvous, or points of refuge along the American coast from which they could launch attacks. A second set strengthened coastal cities against attack. Military engineers placed these fortifications as far downstream as possible from the cities they defended, forcing an enemy to land troops at a significant distance from the city. Sited on strong defensive positions in marshes or rocky areas, the fortresses of the "Third System" used natural barriers to protect their landward approaches.

Fort Delaware was one of the forts built under the Permanent System. When completed in 1859, Fort Delaware represented the largest masonry fort in the United States. But only three years later, on April 11, 1862, Fort Delaware and the other masonry forts of the Third System were rendered virtually obsolete when Union artillery from rifled cannon breached the walls of Fort Pulaski in Georgia. Considered the most impregnable of the large forts, Fort Pulaski fell in just a day and a half. According to a foreign engineer who served with the Confederacy in Mobile, Alabama, masonry forts could not withstand the firing power of modern artillery and would prove inadequate for coastal defense if an attack came in the form of a large Fleet armed with the new technology.

4

POST CIVIL WAR ERA

The forts constructed in the wake of the Civil War needed to address this new coastal artillery technology, and many were built to accommodate it. Developments in this technology during the late-nineteenth century included the introduction of the rifled barrel, the first large-scale use of steel for guns, and the introduction of propellants more powerful than gunpowder. Taken together, these were the greatest advances in artillery since its invention in the fourteenth century.

Conceived during the 1850s, rifled barrels employed long spirals on their interior surfaces that imparted a spin on projectiles, providing a flatter trajectory, greater range, and higher muzzle velocity, all of which contributed to the accuracy of the weapon. A second development involved the building materials used in cannon. Cast iron, the material used earlier, proved too brittle if it cooled too slowly or quickly after casting and proved inadequate even with new improvements in the casting technique. The answer lay in the use of steel. Although steel existed as early as the eighteenth century, the ability to produce large quantities of this high-grade material, and then work it into usable components, eluded armament manufacturers until the later part of the nineteenth century. With an ample supply of pure steel and a collection of the most massive machinery ever created, after 1850 or so, armories could produce gun tubes weighing more than 100,000 pounds.

The third and final development involved developing a powder, or propellant, to cast projectiles distances of several miles. Black powder, composed of saltpeter, charcoal and sulfur, served as the propellant throughout most of the nineteenth century, yet provided the needed force through deflagration rather than by a true explosion. To propel the increasingly large projectiles of nineteenth-century weapons, a propellant that generated immense pressure was needed. The development of cordite, which combined the fast ignition properties of guncotton and the firepower of nitroglycerin and petroleum distillates, provided the propellant powerful enough to eject the larger projectiles. By 1900, new technology provided the Army with the metals, propellants and designs with which to enter the twentieth century.

After the Civil War, changes in the design of coastal fortifications occurred rapidly, incorporating many of these advances in artillery technology into the new facilities. Utilizing a combination of earthen works and concrete emplacements, the post-Civil War fortifications, often provided support to the all-masonry fortifications of the Permanent System Era. Built in 1864 in the vicinity of Fort DuPont, Ten Gun Battery took some of this new technology into account. Built to support the chief fort on the Delaware on Pea Patch Island, known as Fort Delaware, Ten Gun Battery consisted of heavy earthen works on its front with a trench and palisade on its three landward sides. Almost 250 feet in width, Ten Gun Battery contained a heavily reinforced magazine, parade ground, kitchen, and quarters for both officers and enlisted men. The battery's design called for the installation of six ten-inch Rodman-type-Columbiads and four fifteen-inch guns of similar design. The massive rifled guns, weighing nearly 50,000 pounds and stretching almost sixteen feet in length, launched a 300-pound projectile over two and a half miles. The military importance of Ten Gun Battery declined with the surrender of the Confederacy, and the installation, despite its incorporation of some of the new technology, was abandoned by 1870.

ENDICOTT ERA

By the 1880s, in spite of improved coastal defenses, such as those at Fort Delaware and the supplemental batteries at the sites of Fort DuPont and Fort Mott, many civilian and military leaders in the United States considered important urban areas virtually defenseless because of rapid developments in the power of

6

Aerial photo of Fort Delaware
(Courtesy of Delaware Division of Parks and Recreation
Cultural and Recreational Resources Section)

artillery, especially that of the new steel hulled warships. In response to these concerns, the President appointed the Endicott Board in 1885 to assist the Corps of Engineers with the design and implementation of a new system of defense. The program presented by the Endicott Board in 1886 called for a large number of "fortifications which included armaments of the heaviest rifles mounted on disappearing carriages... all of which were to be protected by massive works of reinforced concrete." Congress passed legislation based on these recommendations that authorized the construction of the fifth generation of forts, known as Endicott Period Forts (1886-1905); Fort DuPont, officially commissioned in 1898, was one example of these forts.

Realizing the urgent need for a system of coastal defenses that matched the firepower of the world's navies, the Board proposed a system of seacoast fortifications that utilized the latest in weapons technology as well as the most advanced civil engineering of the time. Steel guns of eight-and twelve-inch bores mounted on disappearing carriages and installed in concrete structures offered the greatest chance of defending the nation's coast from attack. The concrete structures of these batteries served a dual purpose. First, they offered protection to the gun's crew and to the ammunition stores in reinforced magazines. More importantly, the immense weight of the rifles and the intense backward force, or recoil, of these weapons when fired required a substantial mounting platform. To provide additional protection from naval assault, earth or sand served as fill. While these large rifles proved effective against vessels at long range, other weapons could be brought to bear in the event a fleet managed to successfully steam upstream. Rapid-fire rifles and mortars were an integral part of the Endicott period fortifications.

In the closing years of the nineteenth century military engineers undertook the most ambitious building project yet for the protection of the Delaware River. In preparation for the building of a modern masonry fortification to replace Ten Gun and Twenty

Gun Batteries in 1897, the outmoded guns were removed. In 1898 the site was formally commissioned as Fort DuPont; in 1899, construction began on the new fortifications, which were completed in 1902. It was one of the few Army installations named in honor of a naval officer, Admiral Samuel Francis DuPont, a Delaware hero of Civil War fame. When construction of the fortifications was completed in 1902, there were two eight-inch and twelve-inch breech-loading rifles and sixteen twelve-inch breech-loading motors. The completion of the concrete gun and mortar emplacements with their armaments installed was only the first step in the completion of Fort DuPont as a coastal fort of the Endicott period. Unlike the self-contained stone fortresses of the earlier era, the gun and mortar emplacements of the Endicott forts were part of and supported by a larger traditionally laid out military reservation. Remaining after 1902 was the acquisition of additional land, the laying out of a land plan and construction of permanent buildings and supporting facilities. The physical fabric of Fort DuPont was largely completed by 1915. Additional improvements to Fort Delaware on Pea Patch Island consisted of the installation of three twelve-inch disappearing guns. Fort Mott, near Finn's Point on the New Jersey shore, also became a major battery with three twelve-inch disappearing guns of its own.

TAFT ERA

Military technology continued to change and improve during the twenty years of Endicott era fortification construction. In 1905, President Roosevelt charged Secretary of War William Howard Taft with bringing the Endicott plans up to date. Unlike previous defense programs, the Taft Board did not contribute much in way of new fortification architecture. Their recommendations centered on the modifications of extant fortifications, particularly electrification and communications. New developments in electric-based technology such as searchlights, powered ammunition handling, fire control and communications were incorporated into extant batteries and new fortifications in Cuba, the Philippines, and the Panama Canal.

Although few fortifications were built during the Taft era, this period marks significant trends in military technology and serves to bridge the differences between Endicott period and post-World War I period fortifications. The most significant contribution the Taft Board made to seacoast fortification development was the new fire control system. The new method employed "optical instrumentation of great precision, the rapid processing of mathematical data, and the electrical transmission of target sighting and gun pointing information." The system applied a technique known as triangulation that utilized two or more sightings through mathematical computations. By tabulating the successive angles of the target relative to the station, and factoring in elements such as ocean current, wind, computation time, and ordnance firing time, plotting rooms could submit accurate coordinates for fire to the battery. This tactic continued in use well into the Second World War.

The turn of the nineteenth century also signaled the development of the Army's Artillery Corps. Important because it marks the beginning of the distinction between different types of specialized armament used in the U.S. military, the Artillery Corps history spans the first half of the twentieth century; from Endicott-era to WWII-period (Modernization program) fortifications. In 1901 the Army established the Artillery Corps with 126 companies dedicated to heavy artillery and 30 companies to light artillery. The Artillery Corps continued to become more specialized in the years following 1901 and by 1907 differences in the type of armament and technical skills involved with manning the heavy artillery prompted the U.S. Army to officially designate two separate corps: the Field Artillery Corps and the Coast Artillery Corps. The Coast Artillery played a pivotal role in foreign service during WWI and in both foreign and domestic service during WWII.

WORLD WAR I AND POST WAR ERA

The technological advances and armament improvements brought by the Endicott and Taft periods spurred foreign navies to invent better weaponry, and by 1915, several foreign navies possessed ships that outranged the most sophisticated American seacoast batteries. Furthermore, WWI saw the dismantling of many coast defense batteries. The military used the weapons from U.S. fortifications for defenses abroad and the unarmed American bases as training facilities for new recruits.

After WWI, many of the older bases continued to function as training facilities. New 12-inch and 16-inch guns were built and installed in many existing fortifications. In 1922, as a result of the Washington Naval Treaty, the military further secured seacoast defenses with surplus 16-inch naval guns. Mobile guns (tractor and railroad drawn) also provided ancillary support to the older guns. Often permanently fixed on semicircular concrete mounts, 155-millimeter mobile guns (based on a WWI period gun from France) were originally designed as tractor-drawn weapons. Other mobile artillery included both 8-inch and 14-inch guns and 12-inch mortars drawn by rail and tractors.

The military further divided the Coast Artillery into specialized functions during the WWI interlude. The U.S. Army incorporated two new types of artillery, anti-aircraft guns, and mobile weaponry, into the Corps repertoire. The anti-aircraft component became the primary focus of the Coast Artillery Corps by WWII when 3-inch and 90-millimeter anti-aircraft gun batteries became permanent installations at many of the nation's modern seacoast defenses.

The U.S. Army continued to build seacoast fortifications throughout the late 1910s, 1920s, and 1930s. Established on 162 acres near Slaughter Beach, Delaware, Fort Saulsbury represents one of the few post-WWI era fortifications built.

Battery Hall, Fort Saulsbury in April, 2003.
Note the railroad tracks leading into the bunker. Supplies could be
delivered by train to the bunkers.
(Photo by Paul Bauernschmidt)
(Courtesy of Merritt "Sam" Burke, Esq.)

The Army commissioned the fort by 1918 and named the installation after U.S. Senator Willard Saulsbury's father. It was through Senator Saulsbury's proposal that the fortification was made possible. The fort houses two batteries. Each battery, Battery Hall and Battery Haslet, contained two 12-inch guns on barbette carriages. The batteries "were equipped with emergency living quarters as well as storage for the 975-pound, 4-foot-long projectiles, and the 275 pounds of gunpowder required for each firing." The guns from Battery Hall were relocated to Battery 519 at Fort Miles by 1944. Throughout the Second World War, Fort Saulsbury served as a training post and provided tactical assistance to Fort Miles. The U.S. Army officially deactivated Fort Saulsbury in 1946.

Although the U.S. Army built less than twenty-four batteries during this period, advances in seacoast defense weaponry made during this time greatly influenced WWII era fortifications. Through increasing the angle of fire, an Army-manufactured barbette carriage, Model 1917, magnified the range of Endicott-era 12-inch guns from less than eight miles to more than seventeen miles. As cited above, four of these guns were located at Fort Saulsbury and two would be relocated to Fort Miles by 1943. The new 16-inch Army guns and older 16-inch Naval guns provided firing radiuses of 49,100 and 44,500 yards respectively. The increased range brought by these advances proved necessary nearly twenty years later, as the nation prepared itself for another war.

WORLD WAR II ERA FORTIFICATIONS

New developments in carrier-borne and long-range aircraft continued after WWI and by the late 1930s the U.S. Army answered these threats with a new fortification model. The first battery of its kind, Battery Richmond P. Davis in San Francisco, utilized overhead casemating to protect two 16-inch guns, magazines, and operating facilities. This new type of casemating involved the construction of reinforced concrete bunkers. An ample layer of earthen fill and cover was then placed over the casemate. Up to the construction of Battery Davis, substantial guns were not concealed. The concrete walls and ceilings and earth fill provided by the casemate was designed to protect the weapon from large missiles and bombs fired by both boat and aircraft. Battery Davis would come to serve as the model for which all other WWII era fortifications were based.

Events during the fall of 1939 and spring and summer of 1940 served as catalyst to our harbor defense policy. Although the U.S. participated in the war through its lend lease program with England prior to 1941, Nazi aggression on the European continent gained great momentum after the fall of Poland in September 1939. Within ten months of Poland's fall, Germany took Norway, Denmark, and France. Moreover, the Nazi undersea boat, or U-boat, made appearances on America's Atlantic Coast, threatening cargo and passenger ships.

With Germany's invasion of Poland and our peacetime contributions to the British military increasing, many of our military leaders grew concerned about the nation's security. By spring 1940, the War Department questioned the outmoded artillery technology of the Harbor Defense posts throughout the United States and requested reviews and reports of existing coast defenses.

By July of that year, Fort Mott was the only harbor defense post along the Delaware River that was considered no longer required for sea coast defenses, save its "essential areas for fire control or other installations, with access thereto for personnel and cables." Furthermore, the preliminary findings of the study identified major deficiencies in seacoast defense: "fixed batteries of heavy seacoast armament which have served their purpose for the past twenty to forty years are now out-ranged to a marked degree, caliber for caliber, by the guns of modern navies." By 1940 six-inch and eight-inch naval guns had a longer range than the standard post

WWI 12-inch batteries. Moreover, the mobile batteries introduced during and after WWI were meant to provide temporary cover for fortifications not equipped with fixed artillery. Railway artillery, in particular, was extremely susceptible to aerial attack and was not to be used in conjunction with fixed artillery.

WWI brought with it unforeseen destruction and loss of life. America, in the years following the war, aimed to keep isolated from the rest of the world. Within the initial stages of the second World War, however, it became apparent that the United States was sufficiently unprepared for military conflict. The tenuous climate in Europe combined with the inadequate defenses on the country's coastline catalyzed a new and improved military defense program. Termed the Modernization Program, the program sought to rectify the problems enumerated in the study below.

> *The Board considers it urgent that the modernization of the harbor defenses be accomplished at the earliest practicable date. In view of the present disturbed international situation the plans for modernization should seek primarily to meet the present situation rather than to attempt a slower program to meet the indefinite requirements of the distant future. To this end it appears imperative that, for new batteries, use be made of the most suitable guns and mounts now available, or readily procurable.*

The new plan proposed that the military equip existing and new fortifications with batteries of two 16-inch guns as their secondary armament. The program also called for replacement of the tractor drawn 155mm guns with 6-inch fixed batteries, and overhead protection (through casemating or armor shields) of all large artillery. Altogether, the program called for the completion of seventy-seven new batteries that would utilize the newly available 6- and 16-inch Naval guns. One hundred and twenty-eight batteries were to be abandoned (including entire posts) once the new and modified batteries were completed.

15

By September 10, 1940, the modernization plans were approved by the Secretary of War. Military reconnaissance of Cape Henlopen during the fall of that year confirmed the area's highly sought strategic location. By winter 1941, the U.S. Army acquired 1290 acres of the land comprising the tip of Cape Henlopen. Named in honor of General Nelson Appleton Miles who served as a commanding officer in the U.S. Army from 1895 to 1903, the fort was officially commissioned in the spring of 1941. By the time the U.S. Army completed construction, the Cape Henlopen fortification contained two fixed 16-inch Naval guns, two 12-inch guns, four 6-inch guns, four 3-inch anti-aircraft guns, eight 90-millimeter anti-aircraft guns, and two underwater mine batteries. The army removed two railway batteries, each equipped with four 8-inch guns, and two of the four Panama-mounted 155-millimeter guns once Battery Smith was completed.

The completion of the defensive and tactical structures, however, was only one phase of the construction needed for successful operation of a WWII coastal fortification. Unlike fortifications of the past, support structures, military residences, and tactical commands developed alongside the armament. WWII fortifications met the need for fast assemblage in light of the increased tension-laden global environment of the early 1940s. The rapid response to the threat of war mandated that the U.S. use the best armament available at the time, rather than develop new armament to meet the demands of new fortification construction. Therefore, most of the artillery used in the early 1940s existed by the time the modernization program was initiated. The location of the armament often determined where support facilities were built. These batteries were an integral part of the planned military landscape. The addition of standardized barracks, support facilities, and service buildings to the military landscape occurred alongside the construction of bunkers and observation towers. The modernization plan made possible the quick rise to defense the nation desperately needed by December 1941.

The 180-foot Coast Guard Cutter *Gentian*, based at Edgemoor, DE
(Photo attributed to the US Coast Guard.)
(Delaware in World War II Collection. Courtesy of the Delaware Public Archives)

Within the course of four years, the U.S. military completed all of the physical components at Fort Miles.

The forts of the WWII Period represented the culmination of 150 years of military strategy and technology. Building on elements from the past, WWII fortifications utilized technological developments such as open plan design, triangulation, and standardized architecture developed during the Endicott and WWI Eras. More importantly, WWII reservations incorporated these elements into the latest technology readily available. Overhead casemating, artillery shields, and anti-aircraft guns provided the military with the means of defending our coasts against the modern foreign navy. Rendered obsolete within just a few years of its construction, Fort Miles stands testament to the nation's ability to quickly respond to the threats of war. WWII fortifications continued the legacy of incorporating the most powerful guns and the best military strategies available to defend America's coastlines.

FORT SAULSBURY
By C.W. Warrington

Fort Saulsbury is the story of the acquisition and building of a little-known fort on the Delaware Bay, and its life and times during two World Wars. It is, in addition, about the Mispillion area where the fort was built, about the people living there and the part they played in the everyday life of the fort.

This is the true account of the beginning and end of a mighty fort. The characters all lived, and their actual names are used.

DEDICATION

To the military wives' personal and devoted service with unfailing support to make possible their soldier husband's lasting contribution to the Nation and Fort Saulsbury, at this isolated garrison on Delaware Bay.

ACKNOWLEDGEMENTS

The author is indebted to the generosity and eyewitness accounts of the following individuals who contributed to the research and compilation of this material.

Sandy Bea, Newport, Delaware
Stuart L. Butler, Washington, D.C.
Claire L. Warrington, Landenberg, Pennsylvania
Jeanne M. Warrington, Landenberg, Pennsylvania
Keith R. Warrington, Landenberg, Pennsylvania
Augusta Wigley, Slaughter Beach, Delaware

Aerial photo of Fort Saulsbury taken in 2002. Of the four gun emplacements, three are visible just below route 36. To the right are Cedar Creek and Cedar Beach.

ACQUISITION

38° 56' North, 75° 20' West are the geographic coordinates for Fort Saulsbury, a little-known fort six and a half miles east of Milford, in Cedar Creek Hundred, Sussex County, Delaware.

Fort Saulsbury was designed and built during World War I to guard the Greater Delaware Valley against sea attack. One of the greatest industrial power producing and shipbuilding basins of North America, the Delaware Valley ranked high as a target of the Kaiser of Germany. Powder plants, huge oil refineries, and many shipbuilding yards along with ammunition factories, locomotive works, clothing factories, large ports, and many other defense factories all lay in the Delaware Valley.

Therefore, the U.S. Defense Department drew up an elaborate coastal defense plan of the eastern seaboard, which included the defense of the Delaware Valley. Fort Saulsbury was conceived, and, in February of 1917, the United States Government started negotiations for the acquisition of a site for fortifications near the mouth of the Mispillion River, on Cedar Creek Canal. The Secretary of War, Newton D. Baker, authorized the purchase of this property.

The ownership of the required land was divided mainly between two owners, David W. Shockley and Mark H. Shockley. An option covering the transfer of the David W. Shockley farm was secured and the acquisition of this land was accomplished. In June of 1917, David W. Shockley gave immediate possession of his entire farm and buildings, comprising a farmhouse and three barns, including compensation for damages to a standing crop of wheat, to the United States Government. Because of the excessive price asked by Mark H. Shockley for his holdings, however, acquisition of that land by condemnation was instituted. The War Department, Office of the Chief of Engineers, U.S. Army, on June 12, 1917, issued a letter to the Secretary of War, Subject: Cession of Jurisdiction. (See appendix A, p. 143)

Lieutenant Colonel Mark Brooke, Corps of Engineers, U.S. Army, Old Federal Building, Sixth and King Streets, Wilmington, Delaware, was the District Engineer for Fort Saulsbury, and all allotment "Sites for Fortifications and Seacoast Defenses," of Delaware passed through his office in Wilmington. Colonel Brooke reported to Brigadier General W. M. Black, Chief of Engineers, U.S. Army, Washington, D.C.

Mr. William Watson Harrington, Attorney at Law in Dover, Delaware, was recommended by Senator Willard Saulsbury Jr., and accepted by the War Department to enter into contract to "secure options," conduct negotiations, examine titles and perform such other services as were necessary to enable the Chief of Engineers to purchase about 151 acres near the mouth of Mispillion River for fortification purposes. He instituted condemnation proceedings, secured clear titles to all land and acted as a specialist in obtaining expert testimony to establish the true value of the lands and the transfer of title to the United States. Mr. Harrington was paid five hundred dollars for his services.

The David W. Shockley property was purchased for $9,500 and the deed was conveyed to the United States. Steps were taken for the immediate seizure of the Mark W. Shockley farm by institution of condemnation proceedings in July of 1917.

When such property is acquired in time of war, immediate possession may be taken to the extent of the interest to be acquired and the lands may be occupied and used for military purposes, providing that no public money shall be expended upon such land until the written opinion of the Attorney General shall be given in favor of the title, nor until the consent of the legislature of the state in which the land is located has been given. (Appendix B, p. 147).

The Secretary of War sent the Governor of Delaware, John G. Townsend, a draft of an act ceding to the United States; jurisdiction over the land to be acquired, with the request that the recommend to the legislature of Delaware the passage of legislation granting the consent of acquisition to the United States, land at the mouth of the Mispillion River on Cedar Creek Canal. Addressed to the Governor of Delaware. (Appendices C and D, pp. 148-149)

THE PLANT

With the acquisition of the land, construction of the plant required in connection with the 12-inch long-range emplacements for the defenses of Delaware Bay was begun.

The cost of all materials used for construction of these two batteries, each battery having two guns, was high, owing to the difficulty of transportation. The batteries were located at a comparatively inaccessible site, about six and one-half miles, by a poor country dirt road, from the nearest railroad siding and about a mile from the Delaware River on a small creek having a depth of only four feet at mean low water. The lack of water in Cedar Creek and at the mouth of the Mispillion River allowed transportation only by small barges. Towing and handling in the open waters of Delaware Bay was expensive and hazardous, due mainly to sudden storms.

The Rickards Dredging Company of Philadelphia was hired at $80 per day to dredge a channel in Cedar Creek for the purpose of gaining access to the site of the fortification work. A deposit of sand and gravel was also discovered at the mouth of Cedar Creek and was dredged for use in the construction plant. The dredge was put to work on several small deposits of gravel near the mouth of the Mispillion, but it was found that gravel did not exist in sufficient quantity. The deposit evidently came from small clay and gravel reaches farther up the stream, which contained a small percentage of gravel. Sand could be obtained, but the quantity involved did not justify the expense of operating a dredge and washer.

The tug, *Camden*, from the United States Engineers, Philadelphia, PA, towed the Rickards Dredging Company's Dredge Number One to the Mispillion River and after twelve days, when the work was completed, it was towed back to Cooper's Point, Camden, New Jersey.

On August 23,1917, the Charlestown Sand and Stone Corporation was awarded the contract for furnishing and delivering of cement, sand, gravel, and stone to Fort Saulsbury for the construction of fortification works. (See appendix E p. 150-151). In January of 1918, the United States Government took over and operated the Pennsylvania Railroad Company. In April, 1918, the United States Railway Administration put in effect new and increased freight rates on cement and gravel. Charlestown Sand and Stone Corporation had bid before the rates were increased, and this rate increase caused them considerable financial loss. In March of 1919 they submitted a claim for adjustment from the U.S. Government for the excessive freight paid. The Government, however, claimed the contract did not provide for any additional payments above the contract prices, and that their claim could not be entertained by the War Department.

Charlestown Sand and Stone had tried to withdraw from the contract in 1917, but the War Department would not permit withdrawals for any purpose after April 6, 1917, the date of the declaration of war with Germany. The work was completed on March 21, 1919, and the excessive freight amounted to $12,385.99.

The cost of the materials called for amounted to $253,000 for sand, gravel and cement. "Saylor's Portland Cement," manufactured by the Copley Cement Company of Copley, PA, was substituted for "Security" brand cement. The delivery of materials was by motor truck from Milford, Delaware.

An allotment of $150,000 to cover hiring of labor and maintenance was made available from the appropriation for "Gun and Mortar Batteries Act of July 15, 1917" (battery construction), to cover the cost of the plant. An approximate estimated cost of the 12-inch batteries was $870,155.

25

Jones & Laughlin Steel of Philadelphia, PA, was awarded the contract to furnish and deliver 402.83 tons of steel to the Fort.

The overseer of the construction at the Fort was Patrick J. Nealy from the Second New York District Engineer's Office. Mr. Nealy's salary, as foreman, was $149.99 per month. The rate of pay was slightly higher than what he received in the New York District, but it was impossible to get men to remain at Fort Saulsbury because of the isolated location, so it was necessary to pay higher rates to all workers.

Steel sheet piling was considered for use in the fortification, but it was discovered that new sheet piling was impossible to buy due to a priority on work in connection with lock construction and repair projects which could not be carried on practicably without use of steel sheet piling. Timber piling was then used for the fort in place of steel, and this proved successful.

The anchor bolts for the 12-inch long-range guns were special, and strict specifications were placed on their manufacture. The award was made to the McClintic-Marshall Company, Pittsburgh, PA. Bethlehem Steel Company furnished the steel to McClintic-Marshall Construction Company.

Each anchor bolt had nuts and an anchor washer. There were 96 bolts, 2¾ inches in diameter, 100 inches long, each with 3 nuts and 1 washer, and 48 bolts, 2¾ inches in diameter, 87½ inches long. The total weight of bolts, nuts, and washers was about 35,270 pounds. The anchor bolts and nuts were of soft, open-hearth structural steel. The anchor washers, at 12 inches square by 1½ inches thick, were of steel boilerplate and tapped for the bolt thread. Each finished bolt was stamped with the melt number. The tensile strength limit of elasticity and ductility was determined by test pieces cut from selected bolts.

Ultimate tensile strength was from 56,000 pounds to 64,000 pounds per square inch, elastic limit not less than one-half the ultimate strength, the minimum elongation 25 percent in 8 inches and the minimum reduction of area at fracture 50 percent. The bend test was made upon test pieces cut from a selected bolt and machined to one inch square in cross section and bent cold 180 degrees flat on itself, by blows, without fracture on the outside of the bent position.

The cost was $20.21 unit price, or $1,940.16 for 96 anchor bolts, 100 inches long, with nuts and washers and $18.75 unit price or $900 for 48 anchor bolts 87½ inches long with nuts and washers. The finished bolts, nuts, and washers were free from injurious seams, slivers, and flaws and were machine-finished and delivered F.O.B. (Free On Board) to Milford, Delaware.

Watson Malone and Company supplied lumber for the fort, about 129,000 feet, for $5,808.25. The Jones and Laughlin Steel Company supplied the steel for the concrete mass above the foundations, about 402.83 tons, at $84.50 per ton. The remainder of the steel, about 99.5 tons was from the Trussed Concrete Steel Company, at a price of $97 per ton F.O.B. to Milford, Delaware.

The contract for two concrete mixing plants was granted to the Ransome Concrete Machinery Company of Philadelphia, PA, for $3,035.15, and J. Jacob Shannon & Company, also of Philadelphia, for $1,595. The Ransome Mixing Plant had a capacity of one cubic yard of mixed concrete, a hoist tower of 120 feet, steel construction complete with hoist bucket, adjustable hopper with operating platform, and the necessary spouting to reach a horizontal distance of 260 feet. The Shannon concrete mixer had a capacity of one cubic yard with a steam engine, a fixed batch hopper with lever-controlled doors, and an automatic water-measuring tank mounted on skids.

Some of the cement, steel, lumber and miscellaneous supplies were shipped from Philadelphia by river steamer, which made two round trips per week to Milford. The steamer had a capacity of about 200 tons. Materials were unloaded on the Mispillion Lighthouse reservation and hauled over the government road one mile to the fort's site. Some materials were unloaded onto self-propelling lighters, and then brought up Cedar Creek to the site at a point about 1500 feet from the work. The road was a light shell road, in bad condition, over marsh for the entire distance.

The Mispillion River empties into Delaware Bay about 52 miles below Wilmington at a point where severe weather was liable to be encountered during Northeast and Southeast winds, making unloading of supplies hazardous and uncertain. The limiting depth at the mouth of the Mispillion was four feet at mean low water in 1917.

Some deliveries were by railroad to Milford, the nearest railroad point. They were then transferred to light draft barges, and then towed by a seagoing tug over a winding, tortuous course to a point off the mouth of the Mispillion River about 14 miles from Milford. There the barges were anchored and picked up by a light draft tug and towed another mile from the mouth of the Mispillion River via Cedar Creek wharf, the point nearest the site.

Arrangements were begun for a right of way over five private properties for construction of a railway line from Milford to Cedar Beach to be built by the Pennsylvania Railroad at a cost of about $95,000. However, until this rail line could be built, the only practical method, and the one most used was by motor truck from Milford to the work site, a distance of about seven miles over an unimproved public country road.

There was an ample supply of lumber and supplies, at reasonable prices, in Milford for construction of bins, quarters, forms, etc., which were delivered by truck.

Mispillion Lighthouse by Henry L. Jacobs

A small automobile with a business body for use in carrying passengers and light delivery between the work site and the town of Milford was purchased for $650. A two-ton White Corporation motor truck with stake body was also purchased for $2,800.

In order to get labor to stay on the job at this isolated locality, it was necessary for construction of a work camp to establish and maintain the necessary quarters, messing, bathing facilities, and subsistence. The waiver of the eight-hour day and the authorization to pay time-and-a-half for overtime enabled a sufficient supply of labor to be obtained but, because of the difficulty of obtaining labor, due to high local rates in Milford and the vicinity, a work contract was required. No work was done on Sundays or on days declared by Congress as holidays for *per diem* employees of the United States except in cases of emergency, and then only with the written consent of the contracting officer; nor was any work done at night unless authorized in writing by the contracting officer. No subcontractors were recognized and convict labor was prohibited. The camp was so located that buildings were available for occupation by troops upon completion of the work.

Quarters were built-kitchens, mess rooms, toilets for 100 men (white and black), a field office building, store houses, a blacksmith shop, an oil house, two cement sheds, coal and stone bins. A sewer to Cedar Creek and a wharf on Cedar Creek were also built. Permanent walks, gutters, and about one-half mile of permanent road was also built. The sewer line was incorporated in the permanent sewer system of the post. A mess hall, storehouses, latrines and bunkhouses were also available for use by the garrison. Two 60 horsepower boilers with feed pumps and a 10,000-gallon water tank were installed 40 feet above ground, connected with a supply pump by a 4-inch wrought iron main.

Analysis of water samples taken from the well on the Shockley property, purchased for the site of 12-inch batteries, and from another well in the vicinity and from an artesian well said to be

180 feet deep near the drawbridge over Cedar Creek, showed that they were entirely unfit for domestic or steam boiler use due to bacterial contamination. An artesian well near the site of the 12-inch batteries was sunk at a depth of 180 feet and it gave a sufficient supply of suitable water. The cost was $4 per foot for a 4½-inch pipe and $5 per foot for screen placed at the bottom of the well.

C. R. Simpson of New York City was awarded the contract for buildings and concrete construction. The contractor was responsible for all safety of his employees and any damage or injury done by or to them from any source or cause, and was required to discharge any employee who was objectionable or incompetent.

The lumber used was pine and oak, available in the local market. "Stock doors and sash" were used and screen doors were provided on all doorways. The hardware was a cheap grade of cast and wrought iron carried in stock by local dealers. Two-ply rubberoid roofing material was used on roofs as well as sides of buildings.

A plank road about 1,900 linear feet long and 10 feet wide of 3-inch oak was laid on the surface of the ground on four longitudinal stringers 3 by 8 inches imbedded in the ground. Planks were spiked to the stringers with 5-inch spikes. A wood boardwalk was also built.

All closets and basins were provided with trap and roof ventilators. The Speakman Supply and Pipe Company of Wilmington, Delaware, manufactured the lavatory, closet, and shower plumbing. The closet had a wooden low-down tank and oak seat in lid, "BOCA." The lavatory was enameled iron 16 by 19 inches complete with hot and cold basin cocks.

There were four one-story rough frame bunkhouses 24 by 32 feet, unfinished inside. There was one mess hall 25 by 61 feet with an attached kitchen 18 feet 8 inches by 36 feet 8 inches with both rough frame structures unfinished inside and only one-story high. There were also two one-story latrines 16 by 20 feet unfinished inside with each providing four shower baths, four closets, and six lavatories.

A blacksmith shop 16 by 24 feet was built with a concrete floor 8 inches thick. An oil house, ten by twelve feet, frame construction with heavy barn door latches and a storehouse 16 by 30 feet, also of frame construction, were erected. An office building 18 by 34 feet one-story frame with roof and sides covered with 2-ply rubberoid was finished inside with partitions and ceiling of tongue and grooved beaded boards. The floor was laid double with building paper between the two layers. Two cement sheds, each 16 by 50 feet, were constructed with the floor about 5 feet above ground level. Many buildings were occupied by troops or made use of for emergency purposes before final completion.

A trolley system was installed in the batteries to move 12-inch shells. Electric lighting, underground conduits and 25 kilowatt gas motor sets were installed inside the batteries.

The towing of coal barges to Fort Saulsbury was done by a tug of the Philadelphia district. The tug was of such draft that it could only approach within one or two miles off the mouth of the Cedar Creek. It was necessary to have barges transferred from tug to light draft gasoline towboats, which then towed to the site of work.

The tug *Kard* from the Delaware Dredging Company was chartered for the purpose of towing coal scows from Fort Mifflin to the new fort. The tug was one of the few on the river that had sufficient power to tow in the open bay and was of light enough draft to enter Mispillion and Cedar Creeks and, by using this tug, the dangerous transfer in the open water of the bay was obviated.

Photo of Battery Hall, Fort Saulsbury, April 2003, with the
property's owner, Sam Burke standing at the entrance.
(Photo by Paul Bauernschmidt)
(Courtesy of Merritt "Sam" Burke, Esq.)

Thirteen tons of cast iron stairways and fixtures, 15 tons of steel doors, shutters, and gates were used in the construction. Over 60,000 cubic yards of sand and earth were used to cover the batteries to soften any direct hit from enemy shells. To reinforce the concrete batteries 502.34 tons of structural grade open-hearth process, square ribbed "billet" steel concrete reinforcement bars were utilized. Adequate quarters and a winter kitchen were provided with a sunken walk connecting the two-barbette carriage stations in each battery.

The range data mechanical indicator tunnels were raised 4½ feet above the norm because it was found that the ground water stood several feet above the approved level of the bottom of the tunnel and, at that depth, there was a thin stratum of fine saturated sand approaching the consistency of quicksand. It was impossible to keep ditches open at that depth, so the construction of the tunnel at that grade would require the use of pumps to keep them watertight. This caused a slight reduction in space in the storerooms on the flank of the batteries due to running the indicator shafts diagonally across one corner. Since the tunnels were raised, it was necessary for additional protection to give the outer ends of the tunnels additional concrete and fill to compensate for the loss of protection due to bringing them nearer the surface. However, this compensation in protection was not sufficient to take care of direct hits on the tunnels. The radial bars in loading platforms were designed mainly to prevent shrinkage cracks and temperature stresses in the concrete. A ring of concrete 5 feet in depth at the outer edge of the 18-inch platform, with steel on the upper side of the platform and bent down into the 5-foot outer ring, was designed to reinforce the gun block against any lateral movement due to recoil.

Transportation of the big guns was a function of the Quarter Master Department. The guns were made and shipped from Watervliet Arsenal, New York.

12-Inch 1895 MI Barbette Carriage, Model 1917 Coastal Defense gun at Fort Saulsbury
(Photo courtesy of Augusta Wigley)

The 12-inch gun, Model 1895 M.I. for B.C., Model 1917 was shipped in three packages.

No. 1-Gun weight 113,080 pounds
No. 2-Box parts, weight 1,648 pounds
No. 3-Box parts, weight 357 pounds

The Engineering Department accomplished the transfer and mounting of armament. Timber for unloading the guns from barges was assembled on Cedar Canal at the drawbridge at Cedar Beach, which was about 2500 feet from Fort Saulsbury.

It was impossible to transport the guns from Milford, Delaware, to Fort Saulsbury, a span of about seven miles, since the road was in poor repair. Therefore, it was necessary to transport them by water on light draft barges, as the depth of water in the Mispillion River was only about four feet with a rise of tide of about four feet. Also, there were no facilities for the transfer of these guns from railcars to barge at either Delaware City or Wilmington.

The four 12-inch guns, Model 1895 M.I. Barbette Carriage, Model 1917 Coastal defense guns of the United States Army Eastern Defense Command, were mounted and set in concrete. One never heard the sound of active fire except for a few settling practice rounds. However, the guns were maintained and ready for hostile action at any time.

THE FORT

The fort, often mistaken for a location near Salisbury, Maryland, was named in honor of Willard Saulsbury, Attorney General of Delaware, United States Senator and Chancellor of Delaware.

Senator Saulsbury achieved notoriety for his pro-South views during the Civil War. The Senator was a political enemy of President Lincoln, calling Lincoln the weakest man ever to hold high office and hoping that Delaware would remain a slave-holding state.

Later, as Chancellor, he had many accomplishments benefiting the State. His record of achievements in both Federal and State Government was enough for his son, also a United States Senator, to push through a bill to establish Fort Saulsbury in 1917.

The fort was a station of the Coast Defenses of the Delaware (Middle Atlantic Coast Artillery District) of the Second Corps Area. Fort DuPont, Delaware, was headquarters for the sub-district of the Coast Defenses, and Fort Saulsbury was one of its sub posts. Another sub post in 1918 was the Coast Artillery Detachment Barracks at Cape Henlopen, Delaware. Soldier detachments were stationed in tents awaiting the construction of the barracks there.

Colonel Brooks, under whose charge the construction of the 12-inch gun emplacement at Fort Saulsbury began, was relieved of duty due to the demand for officers in the field. Upon victory, most of the regular officers of the Corps of Engineers were relieved from duty as District Officers, and the district was placed in charge of civilians as Assistant Engineers who performed the same duties and had the same responsibilities as did the regular officers during the fort construction.

Garrison at Fort Saulsbury, circa 1918. Note the entrance to the bunker in the top right corner. (Photo courtesy of Augusta Wigley)

Fort Saulsbury rapidly acquired the aspect of a regular Army post. In mid-November, 1918, the contractor's force was reduced to a minimum and, from that time on, the work was carried on under the direction of the Constructing Quartermaster.

Under the direction of the Post Quartermaster, construction of buildings continued. A guardhouse, an administration building, more storehouses, a radio shack, boiler house, and an infirmary with an isolation ward were built. A stable and granary building for two mules was also erected. Although no special measures were taken for prevention and handling of fires, all buildings could be reached by lines from fire hydrants in the water system.

The attitude of the Coast Defense Commander and the Post Quartermaster was one of helpfulness and cooperation through the temporary use of men and equipment under their command throughout the construction.

A fire control station for Saulsbury's guns was set up in a little concrete observation building located on the beach not far back of the Mispillion Lighthouse. The fort's gun batteries were named in honor of two of Delaware's Revolutionary Army officers, Colonels John Haslet and David Hall. Although the big guns were never fired in anger, as no German battleships tried to run the Delaware defenses, their presence was both feared and respected by the German Navy.

However, German submarines did appear off the coast of Cape Henlopen in 1917, and the tanker, *Herbert L. Pratt*, was sunk by a German mine near the entrance to Delaware Bay that same year. The subs laid Naval mines off the Delaware Bay by discharging them through the torpedo tubes, and they would drift free-sometimes hit by ships. Most often the mines would beach themselves in the surf.

German submarines, called Unterseebooten, or U-boats, demonstrated the importance of undersea warfare by sinking thousands of tons of merchant ships and passenger liners. Germany's unrestricted warfare was partly the reason the United States entered the war in 1917.

In 1928 a brick barracks capable of housing a detail of 20 men was built with suitable cooking, toilet, sleeping, and recreation facilities for this isolated post. The barracks cost about $20,000. Also, construction of an ordinance shop, a storehouse, and a small two-room semi-permanent structure with barred windows was built.

In November of 1929, the stable and granary buildings were destroyed by fire and, in order to provide proper shelter for the two animals required for the care-taking detachment at this isolated station, authority was granted to construct a combined barn and hay shed without delay in order to overcome this bad situation. The stable was 16 by 40 feet and cost about $1,000. In 1934 there was a great flood that inundated the fort and caused some damage. A dike was built in 1937 to correct the problem of future flooding.

Fort Saulsbury was occupied by a small care-taking detachment of troops soon after World War I. The families of the soldiers lived on the post, and life on the reservation was slow and quiet.

A Gunnery Sergeant, Dorphin C. Wigley, came with his family to Fort Saulsbury after World War I and was in charge of the care-taking detachment. There were seven men under Sergeant Wigley, and they maintained the big 12-inch guns in excellent condition. Officers would come down from Fort DuPont and hold inspection every week. Master Sergeant Wigley was stationed at Fort Monroe before he came to Fort Saulsbury. At Fort Monroe, the Sergeant received the Distinguished Service Medal of Honor for his quick action for removing black powder from a powder magazine that had caught on fire.

Army dependents and visitors to Fort Saulsbury
(Photo courtesy of Augusta Wigley)

41

The Wigleys lived in a house on the fort, now torn down, and raised their son, Jeremiah, there. Sergeant Wigley was stationed at the fort from 1919 to 1937 and, upon retiring in 1937, he moved as close as he could get to the fort to a cottage in Slaughter Beach. Jeremiah Wigley carried on Army tradition and retired as a Major from the Army.

Some of the men who served with Sergeant Wigley were Clyde Fields, Robert Hayes, and Joseph Horvat. Sergeant Horvat retired from the Army in 1947, and in 1960 he moved to Cedar Neck near the old fort. Robert Hayes was stationed at the fort for 19 years and, when he retired from the Army, he also moved to a home on Route 36 not far from the fort.

Duty during the quiet years before World War II, and especially in the winter months at the fort, was described as extremely dull. In 1940, however, extensive work was underway again at Fort Saulsbury under the direction of First Lieutenant Donald R. Morton, Jr. as Assistant Construction Quartermaster. The work included construction of eight new frame buildings, built by Hugh M. Smyth, a Wilmington builder. In addition, a reconstruction of the sewer system and enlargement of the water system, erection of a cyclone fence about the property, and a post exchange building, plus a number of half-buried, sandbag-roofed igloos for ammunition were also constructed. Electricity, provided by "Rural Electrification Administration, Delaware branch" was brought 13 miles from the Eastern Shore Power and Electric Company to the fort.

The guns were readied for war on December 7, 1941, when word came that the United States had been attacked at Pearl Harbor, Hawaii. All leaves, furloughs, and passes were cancelled, and the men stayed up all night preparing to fire. William Graig was the senior officer on duty that eventful day.

Battery B, 261st Coast Artillery, set up two gun batteries at Fort Saulsbury early in 1942. The gun batteries were hidden in the sand and grassy emplacements and established one of the finest records for firing of any Coast Artillery unit along the eastern seaboard. Battery B was attached to the 261st Coast Artillery Delaware National Guard that was Federalized in 1941 and stationed at Fort Miles on Cape Henlopen. Two of Fort Saulsbury's 12-inch guns were rushed to fresh concrete at Fort Miles in 1942.

Fort Miles, late in 1943, was known as prisoners-of-war headquarters for German and Italian prisoners. Some prisoners worked at Fort Miles and were housed at different locations outside the reservation. Many of these prisoners were housed at Fort Saulsbury, where they were sent to work on farms and in chicken factories around the Sussex County area. There were 6,500 men held in Delaware, the last leaving in April, 1946.

Fort Saulsbury was declared surplus after the Second World War, and the two big 12-inch guns that were left were sent to Watervliet Arsenal and scrapped. Then the government put the fort up for sale, and in 1948 it was purchased for private use. The earthwork fort was used as a storehouse for the Leibowitz Pickle Company of Milford for many years and later as a construction yard and storage house.

In 1982, the fort, 152 acres (including a three-bedroom home that once served as military headquarters), fourteen boat docks on Cedar Creek, two concrete ammunition bunkers which were 300 by 100 feet with four-foot thick walls and ceiling, and the remains of the railroad tracks that were built to supply the fort after World War I were again put up for sale by Gerald Kendzierski, a salvage operator who purchased Fort Saulsbury after the war. Wells Realtors of Milford listed it for $850,000. The State of Delaware could have used this old fort for a recreation site, but was not interested. Currently, the fort is owned by Merritt "Sam" Burke.

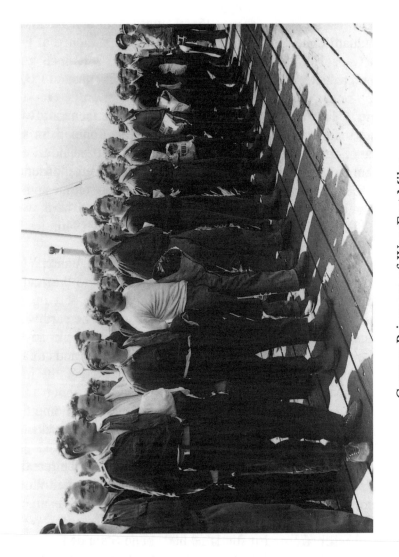

German Prisoners-of-War, Fort Miles
(Delaware in World War II Collection. Courtesy of the Delaware Public Archives)

THE SLAUGHTER

The nearest town to Fort Saulsbury is a sleepy little resort community called Slaughter Beach on the Delaware Bay in Sussex County, Delaware, where in the summer months many residents of Milford and adjoining towns spend their summers.

Slaughter Beach was about three miles long until it annexed Cedar Beach in recent years, adding about another mile to the community. Cedar Beach was so named because of the many wild cedar trees that grow there. Cedar Creek was also named for the abundance of cedars on its banks. Originally, all of the land in this Hundred north of the creek formed a portion of St. Jones County, but in 1683 the names St. Jones and Whorekill Counties were changed to Kent and Sussex. The name Mispillion Creek was substituted for Cedar Creek as the line dividing the two counties.

But how was Slaughter Beach named? Who was Slaughter? No one knows for sure, and no records show anyone by that name owning land in Cedar Creek in the 17th Century.

Legend has it that, around 1640, Indians annoyed people in the Cedar Creek area. The Indians were not hostile but curious of the white man's ways and wares. Tradition has it that the White man tricked them by showing them a mirror. Upon seeing their reflection in the mirror, they thought it was some kind of great spirit. Because of this, they feared the colonists and caused little trouble. However, this did not last long. A man was murdered, and a threat was made to kill all of the colonists. But for an ingenious subterfuge this threat would have been carried out, for the Indians were numerous and could have slain the colonists easily.

A Dutch vessel from Amsterdam had been stranded on the Delaware Bay shore by a low tide. On board was a cannon, an eighteen pounder with large amounts of shot and powder intended for colonists farther up the Delaware River.

About this time, a Swede, who looked more like a half-blooded Indian, came into the settlement. He gave the name Lander and was recognized by some as one who had killed an Indian in the Brandywine area. The Indians vowed vengeance against him.

When a member of the stranded Dutch ship was murdered, whether by Indian or not, Lander suggested the idea of bringing the cannon on shore to keep the Indians in line and probably to protect himself as well.

With incredible toil and assistance from the crew, Lander managed to get the cannon on shore and, when vast numbers of Indians gathered around it, he told them it was a Great Spirit, and it would speak loudly when the Indians did anything wrong.

The gun was charged with powder and fired to prove they had done wrong. At the thundering sound, the Indians bowed down before it and worshipped it, thinking it was a Great Spirit, for no human could speak so loudly.

Then Lander's men charged the gun with shot and made the Indians take hold of a rope in front of the cannon telling them it would punish the guilty for murder. A torch was applied and a tremendous roar sounded along the forest and shore. A vast number of Indians fell dead and dying. Lander and the colonists had placed the ones they dreaded the most nearest the cannon, so they would certainly be blown to bits. Those whom they placed at the further end were not killed and were pronounced good Indians whom the Great Spirit loved.

This story, handed down by tradition over the years, is how Slaughter Beach got its name. (Had it not been for superstitions, such as the cannon spirit, the Indians might have destroyed other settlements along the Delaware Bay.) However, when William Penn's colony was established in 1681, the native inhabitants were treated so kindly and justly that the settlers on the Delaware had no Indian wars during their first hundred years.

There are some historians that do not agree with the legend of the Indian slaughter, but believe that the name Slaughter Beach was for someone named Slaughter who owned land there.

In 1866 William Slaughter, who was postmaster and storekeeper there, established a place called Slaughter Station, just south of Hartly, Delaware. He is said to have built a fisherman's cottage at Slaughter Beach. People in the early 19th Century built shacks along the Bay somewhat like squatters and did not own the land. Mr. Slaughter's cottage could have been one of the first and, at one time, his name referred to the area.

BIG THURSDAY

Big Thursday was begun with an oyster law, passed in 1852, which prohibited the taking of oysters in the Delaware Bay between May 1 and August 10. This was to allow the oysters time to grow larger and produce a more abundant crop.

Because of poor refrigeration, oysters could not be kept for very long, and people who loved to eat oysters the year around awaited the first "R" day with great anticipation.

The first "R" day fell on the second Thursday of August and this day resulted in a great celebration, and it was decided to have Big Thursday every August from then on.

Townspeople and country folk clogged the road with wagons, buckboards, carriages, and buggies and on horseback. Those who had no transportation simply walked with all of their camping equipment strapped on their backs.

People from Philadelphia would go down to Chester and board the steamship for Frederica the day before Big Thursday. The steamship was the *Frederica* that ran from Frederica, Delaware, to Chester, Pennsylvania, and carried both passengers and freight. The fare was $1.50 round trip and meals were 30 cents. The ship entered and stopped at the mouth of the Murderkill River, which was the seat of the little town of Bowers Beach, then continued up inland about three miles to Frederica. Train and stage were also used to bring people to the area.

People who could not find accommodations at the Heartbreak Hotel in Bowers or the hotel at Cedar Beach, or in later years at the Slaughter Beach Hotel, would camp out in someone's yard.

There were many fights at night near the waterfront. Anyone who had a grudge against someone would wait until Big Thursday to fight it out. Many people would go to the waterfront just to watch the fights. Craps games and poker went on behind the sand dunes and up in many lofts. There was a lot of whiskey drinking, and moonshiners did a brisk business.

Many people, however, would come with their children to have fun swimming and fishing, to walk the boardwalk, and enjoy the dances in the evening.

Big Thursday, for Sussex Countians, meant Slaughter Beach, seven miles east of Milford. For Kent Countians, it meant Bowers Beach. The soldiers at Fort Saulsbury also enjoyed the Big "R" day because it broke up the dull life at the Fort.

Big Thursday ended about 1940 when the magic and anticipation of that day left because of the auto. The fun left when the people no longer went down there with wagon teams and stayed the night. It was just not the same with the car. Another reason they stopped having it was because the fights were getting out of hand.

The main reason, however, was a mysterious disease that claimed the oysters. The oyster and fishing industry fell on hard times and, with little else to attract outsiders to the beaches, there were no more Big Thursdays.

Big Thursday has returned to Slaughter Beach in the form of the 4th of July celebration when people come from Milford and the surrounding area by the thousands to watch the annual fireworks display. Boats anchored off shore to watch the show, unknowingly provided a show of their own of many moving lights against the dark night for the people on the beach. The auto that took the fun out of Big Thursday has brought it back for the 4th of July. People can come for a few hours to have fun, then return to the comfort of their own homes. They come during the day to swim, sit in the sun, and walk the beach. In the evening, they build many fires on the beach.

The beach buggies and the four wheel vehicles, trucks and jeeps, along with the ATC (All Terrain Cycles) came for the sole purpose of driving on the beach, mostly at the south end between Slaughter and Fowler's Beach. This pastime is now prohibited by Law to protect the dunes from eroding.

Clam soup, sold at the firehouse, has taken the place of oyster, but the road is still clogged with cars and people. Beer has taken the place of whiskey drinking and fights are rare. People still come to picnic and to have a fun day at Slaughter Beach.

EPILOGUE

Hurricane Hazel caused mass destruction to Slaughter Beach in October of 1954, but the worst storm since World War II was the one that hit in March 1962. A very high tide and wind of over 75 miles per hour caused much more damage along the Atlantic Coast, than it did to Slaughter Beach. But during the storm 35 cottages and 18 trailers were destroyed or disappeared completely. One woman was killed when her home was washed away. If the United States government had not contracted with the American Dredging Company to blow sand on the beach a few months before the storm, the town would have been completely destroyed.

A building standing in Cedar Creek Village, built around 1794, was moved to Slaughter Beach about 1868 and opened as a hotel. The beach had become a summer resort by this time and there were then about half a dozen cottages.

The Slaughter Beach Hotel, set back from the beach in a grove of trees, was destroyed by fire about 1954. Fires in later years destroyed a dance hall center, a stable, and parts of the mile-long boardwalk that had been maintained by the Slaughter Beach cottage owners.

The Artesian wells that serve Cedar Beach and Slaughter Beach are contaminated still with bacteria. Under certain conditions, water with sulfate minerals and a non-harmful sulfate-reducing bacteria will develop a hydrogen sulfide, or rotten egg odor, and can cause black stains and tarnish silverware. A high concentration of Total Dissolved Solids (the total amount of minerals dissolved in the water supply) leaves a white residue when the water is allowed to evaporate. Excessive amounts in the canal can cause a noticeable mineral or salty taste in the water. Treatment of the living organisms of the coli-aerogenes group requires chlorination followed by filtration to remove the residue. To counteract such organic contamination, the well must be cleaned by flushing all casings, then adding chlorine directly to the well. If this does not eliminate the bacteria, a new well must be drilled. During the construction of Fort Saulsbury, it was the decision of the engineers to dig a new well instead of treating the old bacteria contaminated ones, and suitable water was found.

The horseshoe crabs still come in the spring to Slaughter Beach, Cedar Beach, and the Cedar Creek next to old Fort Saulsbury to lay their eggs. Turned on their backs by the tide, some die, thus perpetuating the food chain of hundreds of thousands of shore birds that come to feed on the dead crabs and the newly laid eggs.

Delaware Bay is a staging area for the birds on their way from South American wintering groups to their breeding grounds in the Arctic. They use the bay area to rest and refuel during the long flight north. The horseshoe crabs, or living fossils, unchanged for 250 million years, also provide the food for eels and fish. As many as 20,000 eggs are laid by one horseshoe crab, but if they are laid too shallow in the sand, they are washed out with the next tide to waiting fish.

In contrast, unlike the horseshoe crab that returns every year to Cedar Creek, the Army is not likely to return to Fort Saulsbury.

Horseshoe crabs
(Courtesy of C.W. Warrington)

A MIGHTY FORT CALLED MILES
By C. W. Warrington

A Mighty Fort Called Miles is the story of the beginning and end of a powerful harbor defense fortification. The names of commanders, officers and men stationed there were purposely omitted so no one would be slighted. It is, in addition, about the Cape Henlopen area where the fort was built, about the people living there before the first Europeans landed at this beautiful place, about the men who found it and settled there and the struggles and hardships they encountered. It is the story of the part the cape played in every war since the Revolution and some of the vessels that plied in and around the waters of the Delaware Bay. It is also the brief account of the man for whom Fort Miles was named.

DEDICATION

To the officers and men of the Regular Army, National Guard, Coast Guard, Navy and Reserve units, who served at Fort Miles in defense of the United States against attack in war and peace.

"A task well done is its own reward."

ACKNOWLEDGEMENTS

I am indebted to the eyewitness accounts and generosity of the following individuals who contributed to the research and compilation of this material:

Harry T. Ashcraft, Warrant Officer, Delaware
     National Guard.
Ray N. Bunting, Milford, Delaware.
Robert W. Fisch, Museum Curator, West Point Museum,
     United States Military Academy, West Point, New York.
Charles S. Haas, Newport, Delaware.
Douglas Milligan, Chief Boatswain Mate, Inshore Underwater Warfare
     Division 4-1, United States Naval Reserve, Fort Miles.
A.P. Muntz, Director, Cartographic Archives Division,
     General Services Administration, Washington, D.C.
Jacob A. Parthemore, Sergeant, Delaware National
     Guard, Charge of Officer's Club, Fort Miles. 1942.
Robert Schwabach, Wilmington, Delaware.
Joseph T. Smith, Sergeant, Delaware National Guard,
     Fort Miles.
Horace D. Taylor, Broadkill Beach, Delaware.
Sara S. Temple, Quarryville, Pennsylvania.
Ralph H. Trader, Chief Warrant Officer, Delaware National Guard.
     Supply Officer, Fort Miles, 1942 and 1950.
Theodore C. Warrington, Stanton, Delaware.
     and finally to my long-suffering and patient wife,
Claire L. Warrington.

IN THE BEGINNING

38° 46' 45" North, 75° 05' 30" West marks the location of the once mighty Fort Miles on Cape Henlopen, a sandy point of land where the Atlantic Ocean and the Delaware Bay meet three miles southeast of Lewes and due north from Rehoboth beach in Sussex County, Delaware.

In the year 1610 Samuel Argall, an English sea captain named the point Cape la Warra for Lord de la Warre, the English Governor of Virginia, and gradually the name was given to a bay and river, then a state.

Seventeen years later, in 1627, William Usselin, a Swedish merchant, received permission from Gustavus Adolphus, then King of Sweden, to colonize the area around New Netherlands, and a colony of Finns and Swedes set out. Landing at Cape Henlopen and finding it a pleasant place, they named it Paradise Point. They soon bought from the Indians the land from the cape to the falls of the Delaware River. No settlement was established, however, as these men were interested only in furs.

The cape was at various times called other names: James Cape, Hendricksen Cape, and Cornelius Cape, after Cornelius May who arrived with emigrants from Holland in 1623. Later the name was changed to Henlopen, probably for a Dutch town.

In 1631 a group of Dutchmen headed by Captain Peter Heyes and sponsored by David Pieterssen de Vries, who did not sail with the first expedition, formed a trading company and sailed on the ship *Walvis* from Holland. They landed at Cape Henlopen and called their settlement Zwaanendael, meaning "Valley of the Swans," on the Lewes River near the present town of Lewes. The Dutch settlers mistakenly called Lewes a Place of the Swans because of the wild geese they saw in the marshes.

When De Vries arrived with supplies the next year he found the settlers had been massacred and the fort burned by the Indians. De Vries found the ground littered with the bones of settlers and cattle alike. It may be that the Dutch treated the Indians so badly that they rose up and killed them, or that the settlers ran out of the rum they had been trading with the Indians or refused to give them any more. It is also possible that the local Indians did not kill the Dutch settlers, but that a more hostile tribe visiting the area killed them.

Indians traveled great distances to trade. The Henlopen Indians had little flint for making arrowheads and knives. They were quick to trade with the Pennsylvania Indians, who had found large deposits of jasper (a flinty stone). The Henlopen Indians had salt, clams and oysters to exchange for the jasper. But most of all the Henlopen Indians had shells of all kinds that were highly prized by other tribes.

The Indians of the Henlopen area had been defeated often in the past and were considered "squaws" by more warlike nations. As squaws they were not allowed to carry weapons of war. This could explain why, with few exceptions, the Delaware settlers were spared much of the bloodshed and violence that the neighboring colonies suffered.

Henry Hudson, an Englishman, sailed from Texel, Holland in 1609, looking for a short cut to the East Indies and China on the ship *Half Moon*. He discovered the Great Delaware Bay and Capes and sailed up the bay a short distance. Convinced that this was not a short cut, he put to sea and sailed up the Jersey Coast and on to the river that bears his name. He did not forget about the bay and capes he discovered for he wrote about them and called the river South River and declared it belonged to the East India Company of Holland who had hired him to find a northwest passage to India.

It is ironic that Delaware should be named after a man who never set foot on its soil. It is said that Captain Argall, while serving under Lord de la Warre, was operating off Bermuda when he became separated from the rest of the fleet in a violent storm that blew him to New England. After taking on supplies, he began his return to Virginia by hugging the coast. Late in August of 1610 or 1611, he spied a great bay. Not seeing it on any of his charts, he decided to record it and name it in honor of his Governor.

Hudson and Argall were not the first to discover Cape Henlopen. The Spaniards and Portuguese explored the coastline in the very early sixteenth century, but they did not record the coast too accurately or try to name the cape or bay.

Probably the very first man to see the coast of Delaware was John Cabot, an Italian, living in England when news of the Columbus expeditions reached Europe. With the permission of Henry VII and the financial backing of a group of English merchants, he sailed west to find a shorter route to the East Indies. But he planned to take a route north of the one followed by Columbus. In June of 1497 he reached North America, landing in Nova Scotia. In 1498 he made a second voyage with his son Sebastian, a brilliant navigator, and again sailed west but much further north. He sailed along the West Coast of Greenland and through Davis Strait. He also traveled along the east coast of Greenland, and on his way home sailed south along the East Coast of North America past the Delaware Coast as far south as North Carolina.

This prepared the way for English colonies and gave England its claim to the mainland of North America. The English, a century and a half later, demanded and received the surrender of New Amsterdam and claimed all the territory between Virginia and New England belonged to them because all that coast had been discovered and claimed by Cabot for Henry VII.

The sand dunes of Henlopen and the Great Marsh of Lewes were part of a grant by William Penn to the people of Lewes and Sussex County in 1682. The basic title to the land was a deed from James,

Cape Henlopen sand dunes
(Photo by Jack Goins, Delaware Division of Parks and Recreation,
Cultural and Recreation Services Section)

Duke of York, to William Penn dated August 24, 1682, conveying the land from twelve miles south of New Castle to "Cape Lopen" (Henlopen). "In 1736 Thomas Penn, son of William Penn, made a survey of the lands and decreed that the marshes, timber and feed lie in common for the inhabitants of the town of Lewes and County of Whorekill alias Deale now called Sussex as free liberty for all of the inhabitants of the county to fish, take clams, oysters and cockle shells and gather huckleberries, cranberries and plums on the land as they saw fit, but shall not hunt on the land without consent, and any persons that take up land to be granted a Warrant not to exceed three hundred acres of land to a master (or head of a family) nor a one hundred acre lot to a single person shall pay one single penny per acre or value thereof in a produce grown in the county to the town of Lewes for support of a school for the town."

In 1700 on his voyage from the West Indies the pirate Captain Kidd dropped anchor in Lewes Harbor and engaged in trade with the residents. The colonies prohibited the type of goods Captain Kidd traded the people of Lewes and a number of them were prosecuted by William Penn, via his Court of Sussex County, for engaging in illegal trade.

It is purely legend, but it is said that one night while Captain Kidd was anchored in Lewes Bay he slipped ashore with some of his men and buried a chest of gold in the sand dunes of Cape Henlopen. If Captain Kidd planned to return for his chest of gold in a few years, he might have had difficulty in finding it even on a well-marked map, for the Henlopen Dunes, second only to those found in Indiana, are the fastest moving in this country. Driven by the prevailing sea wind they move inland each year at a rate of five to fourteen feet. The coast moves also and is replaced by ocean. Old maps show the shape of Henlopen not as a hook but as a rounded promontory. The dunes creep inland, covering forests, farmland and even buildings. Sometimes the wind uncovers the stumps of pine and cedar trees buried in the sand for hundreds of years. The Cape Henlopen Lighthouse, constructed by the British to replace a crude wooden building of 1725, originally stood in a pine forest about 1,550 feet inland from the ocean. Shore erosion that dug into its foundation toppled it into the sea in 1926 after a northeastern storm.

The dunes grow as high as eighty feet and, while some are growing others are decreasing in size. The shrubs and the Pitch and Scrub Pines that grow on the dunes of Henlopen are stunted because of the wind and the lack of nutrition in the sand. But the dunes are not a vast wasteland of sand; there are new trees and shrubs springing up all the time. In recent years the dunes have been reduced by the violent hurricanes that sometimes sweep over the cape and, to protect the inland from flooding, the State of Delaware, at great expense, has had to build new dunes and plant Marram grass, nicknamed dune grass, to hold the dunes and start them building up again. In some places, fences, like the snow fences used to stop snow from covering roadways too deeply, are used to build up the dunes. This has worked quite well and the dunes are slowly rising. Grains of sand are blown up the slope exposed to the wind and drop down on the sheltered slope. Thus the dunes gradually advance in the direction which the wind blows.

Not only are the dunes ever moving, but also they are alive with all kinds of odd insects. In addition, cottontail rabbits, field mice, bats and cold-blooded animals such as snakes, toads, tortoises and lizards all live on Cape Henlopen.

The occupants of the Cape Henlopen vicinity when the white man came called themselves "Sickoneysincks" and were part of the Lenni Lenape Nation. The Dutch called them Mahikandeos, and Renappi was the name given them by the Swedes. The French called them Abenakis, but the English gave them the loveliest name of all—"The Delawares."

Early inhabitants of the area were called Lenepid and were believed to have been the forerunners of the Lenni Lenapes who, even to the Indians themselves, were called "The Grandfathers." The Nanticoke Indians also lived in southern Delaware and so did the Assateague Indians who were called "River Indians." All of these Indians spoke the same language, Algonkian.

Lenni Lenape means in Indian language "The Original People." The English told them that the name "Delawares" was the name of a great chief in Virginia. The Indians liked this name because they felt it was a great honor to be called after great chiefs.

They traveled many miles to hunt and fish. The trails they made traveling from one place to another were followed by the colonists and became roads. Some of those trails are now highways.

The Indian would come to the seashore in the summer, much like the vacationer of today, to camp and spend his time in the warm sun and to fish, hunt for clams, oysters and crabs in the bay and store them away for the winter. Some food was eaten raw, some cooked and smoked and still other food was dried or salted.

The Indians obtained salt by putting ocean water in clay pots and letting the sun evaporate the water. They would repeat this operation until a thick layer of salt could be scraped from the inside of the pot. The salt was then used for preserving food or traded with other tribes.

Fish was a staple of the Indian diet. One way of fishing was to use a net made out of plaited grass or vines. Floats of wood were used to hold up the top of the net and stones were tied to the bottom to hold it down. The net was held at one end onshore and the other end was towed in a dugout canoe out into the water and then brought back to shore in a wide circle. Many Indians would then pull the net in and reap their harvest of fish. This method is still used today by some fishermen.

The Indians also used dip nets and traps made of wood splints to catch fish. Spears and arrows were also used on shallow sandbars when fish were plentiful. Black walnut bark was sometimes chopped up and thrown into shallows to catch fish A drug in the bark paralyzed the fish's gills for a few moments. When they came up for air, the Indians caught them in nets.

The Indians living in the vicinity of Henlopen hunted the wild game and birds native to the area. In addition to fish and shellfish they took small whales, turtles, seals, eels and snakes from the sea and marshes.

The worst enemies of the Indian were disease and rum given or traded to him by the white men. The white man brought all kinds of diseases with him to the New World and the Indian had no resistance against them. Whole villages were depopulated by smallpox. Liquor made them act like wild animals. The white man also killed many animals for their furs to send back to Europe. He took land from the Indians and they could not raise crops. Early settlers bought land in Lewes, then called Deale, from the Indians by giving them bright colored coats. With the killing off of the animals the Indians had less and less to eat so they decided to move away from Henlopen. They moved to Ohio and western Pennsylvania. Then when the white man settled in these areas, they moved again, some forced by the government. Today there are Delaware Indians living in Oklahoma and Canada.

There are still people living in Delaware who have Indian blood. There are people who call themselves Nanticokes and others who call themselves Moors. It is said that before the Revolutionary War an Irish lady who lived near Cape Henlopen bought a man slave who said he was from Tangiers, and after some years she became his wife. They raised a large family, which eventually intermarried with the Nanticoke Indians. Their descendants live throughout the State but are concentrated in the Oak Orchard area in Sussex County and in Cheswold in Kent County.

Many Indian artifacts have been found in the Cape Henlopen area. Broken clay pots, smoking pipes, projectile points and other stone tools, as well as shell and animal bones from refuse pits have been found at many archeological sites and provide evidence of the Native American occupation in the area. These sites and the artifacts from them reveal the presence of Native American cultural traditions and lifeways that span many thousands of years.

Salt was an important product in the early days of Henlopen and the early farmers would extract salt from the ocean, but instead of clay pots to hold saltwater they dug holes along the seashore behind the sand dunes on the flats to catch the salt water that flooded into them from storms. Instead of using the sun to evaporate the salt water, they cooked the brine in iron pots over wood fires to evaporate the water. When a raw egg would float on the surface or when a large amount of crystallized salt was noted in the pots it was taken out and put into wooden kegs and stored for future use. Later, salt was shipped to Wilmington and other towns. During the Revolutionary War the Continental Army was supplied with salt from Henlopen. A rude salt-works was established around 1812 and salt was made on the flats beyond the Henlopen Lighthouse. Later most of the buildings were swept away in a great flood called Norman's Flood.

In the days when Delaware was struggling as one of the thirteen colonies for independence there were groups of patriots called "Committees of Safety." They were men who guarded the home defenses and were the forerunners of the National Guard of today.

The Cape Henlopen Lighthouse, built by the British Colonial Government in 1764, was a watch post even before the war started in 1775. Alarm guns were set up at the False Cape, below Henlopen, to signal the approach of enemy fleets. Henry Fisher was one of those patriots who, with a guard of about 30 men, set up a watch post at Henlopen Lighthouse.

Fisher was born in Sussex County and was brought up in a community that was loyal to England. Sometimes he was alone in his support of the colonies to be free states. He became a river pilot in later years and, because of his knowledge of the area and ability as a pilot, it was left to him to choose a site for the lighthouse built on Henlopen. He was employed in later years to make soundings in the Delaware River Channel for the placement of buoys. He established a whaleboat patrol in Delaware Bay and a tight control on other river pilots to keep them from aiding the British.

Fisher's father, a physician, came to America from Ireland before Henry was born and had a large and successful practice, in Sussex County, which left him independently wealthy.

Fisher financed the raising and arming of a militia to guard against Tories, and he almost lost his life to a band of them that invaded Lewes in 1776. His activities on behalf of the Continental Congress earned him the rank of Major in the Continental Army. He maintained constant patrols of the cape and sent the first word of the approach of the enemy's fleet in 1777.

Fisher received commendation for his patriotic support of the Continental Government from the first president of the United States, Thomas McKean. Each succeeding president of the Continental Congress after the adoption of the Articles of Confederation in 1781, signed himself "President of the United States in Congress Assembled." Thomas McKean of Delaware was the first one—he served four months—so technically, McKean was the first president. Washington, of course, was the first elected president.

The British attacked the lighthouse on Henlopen and burned out the wooden steps leading to the tower and destroyed the keeper's lodge in 1779. The light was discontinued until it was repaired by the United States in 1792. Major Fisher died in Pilot Town, Lewes,

Cape Henlopen Lighthouse by Henry L. Jacobs

the same year. In 1812 the light was again extinguished so it could not guide the British fleet into Delaware Bay.

William Penn in his grant to the colony at Lewes permitted only dead timber to be cut out of the pinewoods on Henlopen, but the lighthouse operators were allowed to cut any timber they wanted.

President Washington himself approved repairs to the lighthouse, including a sink and well for water. The Cape Henlopen Lighthouse was a famed landmark that stood for 162 years.

In 1925 the governor of Delaware appointed a committee for the preservation of the old light, and a riprap of stone was placed around the foundation in an effort to save it, but storms washed most of it away.

The lighthouse fell on a bright, clear day with a strong wind blowing a few minutes before twelve o'clock on April 13, 1926. It crumbled into three sections and fell onto the beach.

The old lighthouse was a great tourist attraction, and it was lucky that no tourists were around it when it fell. People used to walk to the lighthouse from Rehoboth and back in those days for a day's outing and picnic.

After the light fell there was some talk of recovering the debris and taking it to Newark where it could be rebuilt on the University of Delaware campus, but nothing ever came of this movement. The old tenant house for the light was burned down sometime later as a safety measure.

The Henlopen Lighthouse had not been in service since 1924. That same year the great lens from the light was taken to the Edgemoor, Delaware, lighthouse station and placed in a frame storage house for refurbishing. It was to be exhibited in a marine exhibit later that year in Philadelphia.

But a few weeks after the Henlopen Lighthouse collapsed the storehouse caught fire and the old lens was reduced to a mass of melted glass.

Storms and erosion washed most of the Henlopen lighthouse away, but a few relics were salvaged and can still be seen at the Zwaanendael Museum in Lewes.

Another happening on Henlopen was in 1936 when the fishermen of the area were hampered by frozen water on the Delaware Bay. They were delighted to discover tremendous schools of live fish flung up by the waves on the beach at Cape Henlopen. The fishermen along with residents of the area gathered up all the fish they could carry and for some time afterwards enjoyed a feast of fish and had plenty to sell neighboring communities. This was called in the press "The Miracle of Fishes."

The Cape Henlopen "Sand Hill," an eighty-foot dune, was used on Easter Mondays for egg rolling. This custom which dates back to early days was associated with Easter because eggs are symbolic of resurrection. But when the terrain became part of the army reservation, the custom was halted and has never been resumed.

Since the bombardment of Lewes in 1813 by the British fleet, the sand dunes of Henlopen lay relatively silent, known only to the wind and tides—to the few fishermen who enjoyed casting in the thundering surf on the ocean side or on the calmer bay side of the dunes. Few people came to view the magnificent scene across the mouth of Delaware Bay or to have picnics and pick blackberries or gather wild beach plums and cranberries in the fall. Cape Henlopen was famous then only as a vast wasteland of peaceful sand dunes basking under the sun.

A MIGHTY FORT

In the summer of 1940 the residents of Lewes began to notice men scurrying over the dunes, looking through telescopes and planting little stakes with red flags.

These men, it turned out, were army engineers surveying the government and state-owned lands. The army engineers had been seen working on canals and breakwater sea walls in the Sussex County area before. But the Army and Navy maintained a secrecy about their operations. However, it leaked out that this was a strategic location for a coastal defense system.

Several months went by and nothing more happened. Then in the spring of 1941, the 261st Coast Artillery, Delaware National Guard, was Federalized and moved into a tented encampment at Cape Henlopen, presumably for harbor and coast defense maneuvers and firing practices. They named their encampment "Camp Henlopen."

Soon derricks and dredges and large road equipment began to appear and, where no motorized vehicle had ever before ventured, a roadway was made, wending its way across the sand dunes. Across the once silent marshes and dunes the sounds of great building rang out.

By this time it was no secret—the army was building a mighty fort on the Henlopen sand dunes. A huge fortress concealed deep in the in the sand dunes, it was to cost approximately $22,000,000 and cover 1,010.8 acres.

The original tract of land was a grant of William Penn in 1682 to the people of Lewes and when the Federal Government paid the State of Delaware $62,046 for the tract there was much litigation as to the rightful recipient of the money.   This tract of

The Main Gate at Fort Miles
(Delaware in World War II Collection. Courtesy of the Delaware Public Archives)

land was known as "Common lands" of Lewes and was left in trust for the people of Lewes and Sussex County.

The fort, consisting of about four miles of beachfront on the ocean and about a mile on the bay, was also called "William Penn's Acres" and, because of grants dating from the seventeenth century, the people of Lewes said the money should go to their town, not the state.

The government condemned private land under a court order through the United States District Court so the fort could be built without delay.

Some of the land in the tract had been ceded to the Federal Government by Sussex County for a quarantine station in 1873. But the land was never used by the United States for this purpose and it was returned to the State of Delaware and became part of the beach lands under the jurisdiction of the State Highway Department.

Then in 1941 the Delaware General Assembly again ceded a portion of land to the Federal Government consisting of 1,500 feet of beach front, 1,200 feet deep from the low water mark, with the condition that the land be used only for national defense or other governmental purposes pertaining to defense.

The 261st Coast Artillery did not leave at the end of the summer but started to reinforce their fifteen pyramidal canvas tents against the coming winter and to continue their firing practice and training.

Then the Navy, taking over the old Lewes Coast Guard Station as a headquarters, moved in and set up the Harbor Entrance Control Post.

Old Lewes Coast Guard Station illustrated by Henry L. Jacobs

The Coast Artillery laid M4 ground mines containing 3,000 pounds of TNT across the entrance to the harbor. These mines, some nine feet in length, were attached to heavy weights to hold them in position. Thirty-five grand groups of thirteen mines each were electrically controlled and detonated from the mine control bunker. The mines were effective from a depth of sixty feet. The mines were laid across the channel from Cape Henlopen and Chicken Shoals some eight thousand yards. The task was intricate and could be dangerous. Three different types of craft were employed to install the mines. A mine planter hauled the mines and cable to the area. The yawl boats connected the cables from the shore to the junction boxes, and finally marked the position of the mines. Small launches delivered the main cable to the shore. The final positions were plotted on the mine control plotting board. Observers in towers tracked the targets, with sophisticated range finding instruments, allowing the commander to detonate the mine at the correct moment.

Underwater defenses of the harbor were layered. At the very entrance to the bay two magnetic strips were installed on the bottom by the navy. These magnetic anomaly detectors registered the passage of any large metal object. Just behind the magnetic strip lay three underwater microphones called hydrophones. The hydrophones allowed technicians to identify the type of craft entering the defensive zone. A rough speed and heading could also be determined by these devices. At night search lights illuminated the area for the benefit of both the mine warfare team and for the artillery men manning rapid fire three inch guns brought in from Fort Delaware and Fort Wadswoth. Harbor pilots worked at least 6 days per week guiding the ships through the mine fields. The mines were inert until fired but it was important to control traffic in the busy water way.

Strategic planners were concerned at the onset of the war that heavy German Battleships might venture night time attacks on the crowded anchorage at Cape Henlopen. To fend off these attacks,

U.S. Army Mine Planter *Frank* used by companies A and B of the 21ˢᵗ Coast Artillery Regiment. (Photo courtesy of Edward W. Cooch Jr.)

heavy gun batteries were planned for Fort Miles in accordance to a modernization scheme developed in the 1930s that would reduce the number of gun calibers from six to just two. "Sixteen's and sixes" described the plan to emplace 16" guns with over the horizon range supported by rapid firing long range six-inch guns.

Two each of the concrete and earth covered emplacements were planned for Fort Miles. While these projects were underway, temporary defenses were moved into position. Eight-inch guns on railroad cars began arriving at the Fort on March 15, 1942. A total of 8 of these very old but reliable weapons were placed in horseshoe shaped epaulments lined with paper cement bags. These installations were very temporary in nature. On the northern end of the cape batteries of 155mm field artillery pieces took up position to deny entrance to the harbor. As the threat from the German surface fleet diminished so did the armament at Fort Miles. The second sixteen-inch battery was scrapped and replaced by moving two of the turn of the century twelve-inch guns to Cape Henlopen constituting battery 519. The rail guns were removed upon completion of the heavy batteries. The 155s departed to be replaced by 90mm anti-motor torpedo boat batteries. The three-inch guns were retained for anti-aircraft duty.

When the Second World War started, the Coast Guard conducted "Search and Rescue" missions for downed aircraft and ships in distress and picked up survivors from torpedoed vessels. They had only an 83-foot cutter, a 38-footer and two 40-foot patrol boats and a small utility surf boat to do this tremendous task, where it was considered a routine job to save lives in all kinds of weather, at great risk to their own lives. The names of the cutters were *Mohawk, Lilac, Zinnia* and *Narcissus*. The Delaware Coast Guard was part of the Fourth Naval District, and was in charge of patrolling the beach day and night throughout the war years. Some walked the beaches with dogs, others rode horses along lonely stretches of the coast.

The Coast Guard wore dark uniforms and rode only black and brown colored horses while patrolling the beach. Light colors would have stood out and they could have been spotted easily. The horses were stabled at Fenwick Island and after the war they were sold at public auction.

The Coast Guard "Horse Marines" unit was started in July 1943 and continued for the duration of the war. When the horses were brought in, most of the dog patrol was discontinued. German spies were known to use a mixture of dried blood and cocaine to cover their trail. This caused the dogs to lose their sense of smell, making them almost useless for trailing.

The Coast Guard used the Lewes station #139 as a central base. Bethany Beach and North Bethany Beach, South and North Indian River and the DuPont home at Rehoboth were other stations. The H. Rodney Sharp home in Rehoboth was used as a barracks and the R. R. M. Carpenter home was used as a hospital for the Coast Guard.

The sailors, just like the army boys at Henlopen, had to live in tents until barracks could be built.

Contractors worked day and night to complete the multi-million dollar defense project. One of the largest construction companies in the East, the White Construction Company from New York, built the giant fortifications. George and Lynch, a Delaware firm, worked in conjunction with White.

Engineers, mechanics, pile drivers, electricians, carpenters, all kinds of tradesmen and laborers were hired to complete the defense project. Many tradesmen flocked to Lewes and the surrounding area for quarters for themselves and their families. Gas was rationed and they could not commute very far after the war started.

Fort Miles temporary tent quarters, ca. 1941
(Delaware in World War II Collection,
Courtesy of the Delaware Public Archives)

The fort, a national defense project being built by the U.S. Army Engineer Corps, was cunningly concealed and protected against any enemy trying to reach the major cities along the Delaware River from the bay.

The new fort was built with a thick layer of sand on top as well as in front of her guns for protection against air or sea attack. The same old defensive theory was used as in past history of coastal defense fortifications: to give the enemy as little as possible to shoot at and use a soft material like sand, dirt and reinforced concrete to absorb the force of hostile bombs and projectiles.

The sand dunes back of Cape Henlopen were the center of the defense system. The fortress guns commanded the peninsula of South Jersey and the entrance to Delaware Bay. The 800-foot wide 40-foot deep channel was mined to stop enemy battleships. The mines did not stretch clear across to Cape May because of the sandbars and shallow water on the north side of the mouth to Delaware Bay. Only the channel was mined because no ship or sub could have passed over the sandbars.

Controlled submarine mines, "Mine Command," protected the river from underwater attack. About twenty men controlled the mine project.

Coast Artillery laid the mines, sinking heavy brackets and attaching explosive charges that could be fired from control stations ashore. Three types of mines were used: timed, electronic and magnetic. The magnetic detector loop installed in April 1942 consisted of six groups of mines with thirteen mines in each group. They were naval mines, Type 51, Model 0.

Searchlights were set up in a straight line across the point. These searchlights were mobile units on trailer beds. At night three lights would scan the entrance to Delaware Bay for the telltale periscope of submarines. Cape May also had three searchlights operated by a

Two World War II fire control towers photographed from the
Delaware Bay.
(Photo by Jack Goins, Delaware Division of Parks and Recreation,
Cultural and Recreational Services Section)

battery from the fort at Henlopen. When a vessel left or entered the bay at night, the lights from Cape Henlopen and Cape May would be concentrated on the mine sweeper that would open the mine gate to let the vessel pass safely through.

The big guns were brought in and placed in the fortress pits. Eight and sixteen inch in size, they had a range of twenty miles or more and could sink a ship far at sea without seeing it. Concealed along a four-mile sea front, the fortress had gun emplacements, ammunition dumps, and living quarters.

Dotted across the Point of Capes were concrete control towers—the only visible evidence of the mighty harbor defenses. A state highway running from Lewes to the sand dunes was closed and a military road made of bedrock was constructed on the two and a half-mile strip. Signs were planted at the entrance and along the boundaries at the new fort and marked "Prohibited." Military restrictions were tightened in the Eastern Military Area, under whose jurisdiction the new fort came, and orders came from the First Army's Eastern Defense Command headquarters at Governors' Island, New York to move all persons considered dangerous to national defense.

The fort was unique, unlike many other army reservations, because it was not visible to motorists from the road. The only road was through the fort and the public was barred from using it.

The fort was also designed to halt any flanking movement that might be aimed across the Delmarva Peninsula from the Chesapeake Bay. Fort Monroe, along with the fleet at Norfolk, protected Baltimore and Washington and the great port of Philadelphia from the south.

Baltimore, the center of the industrial area, was one of the most important ports in the nation and a center for shipping during the

World War. Fort Monroe, with its big guns and the country's largest and most powerful fleet based at Norfolk, Virginia, guarded the Chesapeake area. The Chesapeake Bay was considered nearly invulnerable.

The Army Corps of Engineers supplied hundreds of detailed plans for the gun emplacements. Plans for casemate and central transverse magazines and plotting rooms, electrical system details, power rooms, radiator rooms, fuel storage rooms, and many other plans and maps were all considered top secret in 1941. The bunkers also had dehumidification systems and gas-proofing systems as well as air conditioning and heating systems.

Some bunkers had two entrances and had the name of a gun battery cut into the concrete framing. Some did not. The letters were 9" high, about 6" across and 3/4" deep. On a bunker entrance was the name of the battery, the letters U. S. E. D., for United States Engineer Department and the date—1942. The big 12" and 16" gun batteries were named Battery Doe, Battery Hunter, Battery Herring and Battery Smith. The plans of these batteries are on file in the Philadelphia District Engineer Office (RG 77).

Target plotting changed very little since the turn of the century. In the early war years, target data was collected by observers in the towers lining the shore. These towers worked in groups of three to triangulate the position of hostile ships. This information was sent by telephone to the plotting room, which relayed the information to the gunners. Additional observers reported the shot fall as long or short sending additional data for correction to the plotters. On November third, 1943, Fort Miles activated five SCR-296A fire control radar sets. These radars could part the mist and fog of the Atlantic Coast and gave sight to the guns after dark. Although these sets were rather primitive they could be used individually or in groups to plot targets for the big guns.

Fire Station at Fort Miles by Henry L Jacobs

Coast defenses could be attacked by air, sea, or even land and because they were fixed they had to depend on air and sea support of planes and ships.

Supplies for the fort at Cape Henlopen came over the new highway and the new tail head spur constructed just for the fort. An 1,800 foot-long pier was built so supplies could be brought in by ship. Although a $3,000,000 air base was constructed at Cape May, no air facility was built at Cape Henlopen, but an occasional helicopter landed on the parade ground in later years.

The fort was designed to guard the Delaware Valley against sea attack and, concealed deep in the sand dunes, the huge fortress could have destroyed any enemy trying to reach Wilmington, Chester, Philadelphia or Trenton from the bay. It overshadowed old Forts Mott, Delaware, and DuPont in importance by protecting the vast industrial centers in the Great Delaware Valley. One of the greatest industrial power producing and shipbuilding basins of North America, the Delaware Valley ranked as one of the higher ranking targets for the Axis powers if they had decided to attack America.

Although inland from the river the old Krebs Pigment Plant at Newport, owned by DuPont, was engaged in a secret project called Project XX, making silicon crystals for highly classified radar units, and could have been shelled by a war ship from the Delaware River.

DuPont Company plants at Carney's Point and Gibbstown, the Bellanca Aircraft Corporation plant near New Castle, the huge oil refineries at Chester and Philadelphia, Pusey and Jones Shipyard, New York Shipbuilding, Cramp's Shipyard, Sun Ship, League Island Navy Yard, Pedricktown Ordnance, Baldwin Locomotive Works, Remington Arms, Frankford Arsenal, the large ports, defense factories, clothing and ammunition factories, electrical

Battery 519 as it appeared in 1968
(Courtesy of C.W. Warrington)

factories and machine works and many other industrial plants engaged in defense lie in the Delaware Valley.

Prior to World War Two Coastal gun emplacements lay in the open, vulnerable to air attack. The main armament at Fort Miles was well hidden in steel reinforced concrete bunkers that were covered with earth and sand. These positions were virtually invisible and very well protected. Infantry units were often kept on hand to fend off land attack when threats loomed. Off shore the nascent Civil Air Patrol, as well as the Army Air Corps patrolled for lurking submarines, working in cooperation with the navy.

The onset of war in the Atlantic found the harbor defenses of the Delaware in deplorable condition. Spanish American War era fortifications at Fort Delaware, Fort Mott, and Fort DuPont were all that stood between an aggressor and the industries of the Delaware Valley. Further down river, slightly more modern Fort Saulsbury brushed the dust off their weapons and prepared for a fight. As the new defensive line was drawn in the sand at Cape Henlopen these forts began to close or to serve rear echelon functions. The guns were scrapped or sent to allied countries to enhance their coastal defenses.

Three-inch guns were set up and 6,000,000-candlepower searchlights were used for night firing. The Bethany Beach site south of Rehoboth became the main practice area a few years later when the shipping in the Delaware Bay increased and the anti-aircraft guns were considered a possible threat to shipping.

Then in August of 1941, on the 102nd anniversary of the birth of the late commanding general of the U.S. Army, Lieut. General Nelson Appleton Miles, the army named the new fort on Cape Henlopen. Fort Miles, a regular army post, was born, risen from the peaceful sand dunes of Henlopen, as a mighty harbor defense commanding the entrance to Delaware Bay.

The naming of the fort came as a surprise to the residents of Lewes and other citizens of the State of Delaware who thought it should be named after some Delaware statesman or at least called Fort Lewes or Fort Henlopen. But true to form, and like the early Indians who liked to be called after great chiefs, the Federal Government chose to honor General Miles.

The citizen-soldiers who entered Federal service in 1941 and went into "temporary" bivouac on the sand dunes of Cape Henlopen never dreamed that bivouac would become the best equipped defense installation on the Atlantic Coast, the mighty Fort Miles.

Fort Miles rapidly acquired the aspect of a regular army post. A clubhouse for commissioned officers was built as well as individual day rooms for each battery. A special noncommissioned officers club was also built. Barracks and mess facilities replaced the tents. The barracks were frame two-story structures on concrete foundations. Each provided sleeping facilities for 63 men. Later, concrete block one-story barracks were built.

A ten-bed hospital operated by the 261st and 21st Coast Artillery medical detachments was built. Dental services were also available.

A post theatre was built and movies were shown in the evenings. The theatre also served as a dance hall and dances were held every two weeks sponsored by the U.S.O. and the Lewes Coordinating Committee. An air-conditioning system was added to the fort theatre in the summer of 1942 to the great enjoyment of the men. When the gymnasium was built, dances were held there because attendance had far out grown the post theatre.

Professional entertainers from other army posts and U.S.O. entertainment programs were provided. On dance night the prettiest girls of the nearby towns were bussed in to dance with the servicemen. They were chaperoned of course by matrons from

Entertaining the troops. Sgt. Edward Talent and
Cpl. Joseph "Chubby" Schwarzman
(Delaware in World War II Collection.
Courtesy of the Delaware Public Archives)

Soldiers gather around the piano for rehearsal
(Delaware in World War II Collection. Courtesy of the Delaware Public Archives)

Rehoboth and Lewes. The orchestras were composed of men who once played with "name bands" and provided the best dance music of the time. Even Fort DuPont's fine orchestra was used on occasion.

A chapel was built on a high sand hill overlooking a large part of the fort. Soldiers and sailors of all faiths could worship in this little chapel.

The Fort Miles fire hall was built and supplied with a ton and a half fire truck. The Quartermaster Corps supplied a fire chief for the Fire Brigade.

The Post Exchange was a busy place where a soldier could buy the extra things he needed like toilet articles, ice cream and soda, and 3.2 beer.

Fort Miles consisted of 1,010.8 acres and used 792 acres of it as a training area, including small arms firing ranges. Other buildings included armament and an automotive repair shop, storage bunkers for ammunition and many warehouses.

Many recreation facilities were developed to keep up morale and prevent boredom. A target range was completed and competitive target shooting was established. Shooting was with .22 caliber rifles at 1,000 inches. Later a .30 caliber range was set up with the ocean as a backstop. This range was used also for qualifying tests with military rifles and pistols and was part of the soldiers' training. The qualifying score was entered on his military record.

A contest was adopted for the privates in the early days of the fort. Each month the most outstanding soldier was rewarded with a three-day trip to New York City with all expenses paid.

All Faiths Chapel, Fort Miles
(Photo courtesy of C.W. Warrington)

A baseball diamond was provided and touch football was played quite frequently. In the post gym volleyball and basketball were played as well as many other athletic sports.

Fishing was the chief sport and the sailors and soldiers considered it their favorite form of recreation. Drum fish were caught in 1942 and some of the largest weighed around 70 pounds. Swimming was also a favorite on the reservation's private beach.

Even the wives of the servicemen had their own private club called "The Wives Club of Fort Miles." All wives of servicemen from Fort Miles living in Lewes and Rehoboth Beach and nearby towns were eligible. The Lewes U.S.O. Club entertained them on special occasions at teas and other activities. The U.S.O. also sponsored several jitterbugging contests for the servicemen.

Fort Miles even had its own newspaper. The paper entitled "Shot on Way" was published and edited by the men of the 261st Coast Artillery. The editor of the "Shot on Way" was a private from Wilmington. The illustrations and cartoons would have done credit to any national-newspaper.

In 1944 the government built the new Fort Miles station hospital in the town of Lewes, consisting of 16 long one-story cement block buildings and numerous smaller buildings. The buildings were connected by walks. The 118-bed hospital, built on 16 acres of land next to the Lewes Public High School on Savannah Road, was constructed by White Construction Company on the old Leben Lyons Estate. The cost was $385,800. It served as a hospital base for nearby Fort Miles and other military posts.

Under the Special Service Division of the post a quiz program was initiated to determine the "Wise Old Owls of Fort Miles." Four contestants each represented the various military units stationed at the fort, and the finalist from each unit competed at the end of the week. The quiz was conducted after the manner of the then

Christmas, 1943 issue of the "Sandpaper", one of the base's newspapers

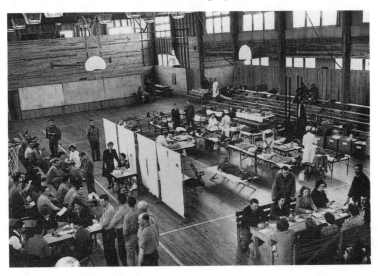

The soldiers at Fort Miles responded to the cartoon above and turned out for the blood donor drive held in the base gymnasium. More than 600 pints were collected for the Red Cross. (Delaware in World War II Collection. Courtesy of the Delaware Public Archives)

famous "Quiz Kids" radio programs. Rivalry was keen among the teams for there was a prize of 60,000 cigarettes and the honor of being dubbed the "Wise Old Owl of Fort Miles." Dictionaries were the most popular books in the post library. Door prizes were awarded and an audience was encouraged with a series of "Jackpot Quiz" questions.

The first Coast Guard Station built at Lewes in 1884 was sold and moved to the Cape Henlopen Beach several years before Fort Miles was built and made into a men's private club. The sturdy structure was taken over by the government in 1941 and since then was the headquarters for the naval contingent on the post, the "Harbor Entrance Control Post."

Because the building was located conveniently close to the fort's main bathing beach on the ocean front, it was equipped as a surf club for the officers and enlisted men of Fort Miles and their ladies and wives and guests. The new club was equipped with two lounges, one for officers and the other for enlisted personnel. Private dressing rooms for the men and their guests were made available. There was also a branch post exchange in the building. The Rehoboth Veterans of Foreign Wars bought it after the war, and in 1949 it was moved to Rehoboth and reconstructed as a VFW Post.

The Maritime Exchange Office was moved in 1942 from a little building on the Delaware Breakwater to the Fort Miles Army Reservation. The exchange is a center for maritime and shipping fraternities. Lewes has not been a great loading port but has considerable importance as a port of call. The Lewes Coast Guard took supervision of the little building on the Breakwater in 1954.

Four barbette carriage 12-inch BC M-1917 coastal defense guns of the United States Army Eastern Defense Command were brought

Sales Store opens at Fort Miles. Mrs. Richmond T. Gibson is
making the first purchase. She is being assisted by her husband,
Col. R.T. Gibson, center, commanding officer, Fort Miles and Col.
H.V. Brunson, acting quartermaster of the Second Service
Command.

(Delaware in World War II Collection.
Courtesy of the Delaware Public Archives)

Boxing match in the Fort Miles gymnasium
(Delaware in World War II Collection. Courtesy of the Delaware Public Archives)

to Fort Saulsbury by barge in 1917 and 1918. Two of these 12-inch guns were rushed to fresh concrete at Fort Miles in 1942. After World War I the fort was not closed but was maintained by a small detachment. In 1941 the government did not have to condemn land to establish a fort as it did at Miles because it was already an army post.

"A" Battery of the 261st, in August of 1941 set up four G.P.F. French 155-millimeter guns on the sand dunes at Henlopen and began firing them for training.

Battery "C" maintained the three-inch guns remaining at Fort Delaware and Fort DuPont, Batteries Hentig and Eldar respectively. Battery Hentig's two guns moved to Fort Miles to cover the mine field and to provide limited anti-air capability. Battery Eldar guns were removed for a very short time to defend the area in front of the Liston Range light.

Liston Point is a point of land 12 miles southeast of Delaware City forming the western point of arbitrary division between the Delaware Bay and Delaware River. The point was named after Morris Liston who, prior to 1680, owned land in the area. It is also called *Hager Udden* which is Swedish for "Heron Point."

Deep in the sand bunkers, where the big guns were placed, were constructed wardrooms, ammo and equipment store rooms, food storage rooms, kitchen facilities and sleeping quarters. The big disappearing guns were hidden behind heavy steel doors. When in action the doors retracted allowing the gunners to perform their deadly work. Ventilation, toilet facilities and communications systems were also installed and, when the steel doors at the entrance to the bunkers were closed, a firing battery could stay in the bunker for months if it had to under war conditions. As each set of guns were sighted in on its perspective ranges, residents experienced shock and awe first hand as the blast of over 300 lbs. of powder shattered windows for miles around.

New six-inch guns were brought in and placed at beach level and test-fired only. These guns were never fired again.

German subs would lay off the entrance to Delaware Bay and sink shipping trying to reach Europe. Mute testimony to this was the debris of sunken ships that washed up on the beach at Miles. One merchant marine from Delaware had six ships torpedoed from under him before he finally reached Europe and then the ship he came over on was sunk on its return trip to the States. But because of the decreasing U-boat activity in late 1944, the two twelve- and two sixteen-inch guns were also withdrawn and the men were moved to Fort Jackson, South Carolina, and Fort Bragg, North Carolina, to a coast artillery brigade. In April of 1945, due to policy of the War Department, the Harbor Defense units were converted to field artillery. A cadre of approximately one hundred men was left to man the fort, and they were assigned to the 21st Coast Artillery Regiment at Fort Miles.

In 1945 Fort Miles was known as Prisoners-of-War Headquarters for German and Italian prisoners. Some prisoners worked at Miles and were housed at different locations outside the reservation. There were 6,500 men held in Delaware, the last leaving in April 1946.

The army stored tons of ammunition in the fort for all her guns. The twelve- and sixteen- and the six- and eight-inch guns had armor-piercing and high explosive shells. There were also tracers, armor piercing, and high explosive ammo for the ninety-millimeter anti-aircraft artillery guns and later the forty-millimeter ack-ack, and of course there were great stores of ammo for the small arms.

The final armament arrangement at Fort Miles, minus the mine fields, remained in place until after the Korean War. At that time the Defense Department began to alter the use of the Fort.

U-858 Commander, Lt. Thilo Bode
(Delaware in World War II Collection,
Courtesy of the Delaware Public Archives)

In 1958 the navy took over the larger gun batteries converting Battery Herring to a SOSUS listening station. The other batteries and their support buildings were converted to recreational facilities for the families of military personnel posted in the region. Some soldiers stationed at Miles during the Second World War referred to the fort as "Delaware's Maginot Line." Similarities were drawn between the Fort and the Line because they were both buried deep in the earth and both were vulnerable from the rear. Some of the smaller guns could have been turned around and used, but the big guns would have been almost useless. It would have been difficult for the enemy to have out-flanked Miles, but it was not an impossibility.

The Maginot Line, in France, was overhauled in the early 1950s for possible use in case of an atomic war. The underground bunkers at Miles are also reserved for select personnel in the event of nuclear holocaust.

Fort Miles continued as an army post and became quite active as a training post during the Korean War outbreak in 1950. After the Korean police action, a cadre commanded the fort again. In the summer, when National Guard and Reserve units moved in for training, the complement was increased temporarily to assist them. The cadre, consisting of about a hundred men, was a regular army unit designed to operate and maintain the fort with the least amount of personnel. Duty during the winter at the fort was described as extremely dull.

National Guard anti-aircraft units taking part in training exercises were from the District of Columbia, Virginia, Maryland, Pennsylvania and Delaware.

The Delaware National Guard had two units that used the fort as home base, Battery D, 280th self-propelled Automatic Weapons Battalion and the 208th Radio-Controlled Aerial Target Detachment.

Then in 1958 the Army decided to close Fort Miles because of the increasing obsolescence of artillery due to tactical missile development. The shutdown of Miles was also an economy move that closed Fort Chaffee in Arkansas and Fort Polk in Louisiana. The estimated cost savings to the government was about $300,000 a year. The Army transferred its military personnel to other bases and found places for some of the civilian personnel.

The Mine Command was taken over by the Navy in 1949 from the Army, which had operated the project for about two years. This was in line with Defense Department orders transferring such projects to the Navy throughout the nation. The mines, however, have been blown up in place.

The Departments of the Army and Navy retained some land at Cape Henlopen for defense purposes. An air defense radar unit of the Navy also remained. Fort Miles became a radar station in the Nike Missile Defense System.

In 1962 the Army declared more than half of Fort Miles as surplus land, and the State of Delaware was given first claim to it rather than some other federal agency. So in April of 1962 the Army turned over to the General Services Administration the disposal of the surplus land.

There was no doubt this time in the minds of the Delaware leaders that Fort Miles would make an excellent state health and recreation area. Recreation areas were beginning to be very much in demand with the rapid increase in population. The cost of maintaining some two hundred buildings on the old post presented somewhat of a problem to the State.

The town of Lewes, however, in 1962 claimed part of the slicing up of the federal pie and the Lewes Chamber of Commerce presented five hundred signatures on a petition to back up the community's claim to part of the land. In 1941 Lewes caused much litigation as to who should be the recipient of the money paid to Delaware by the Federal Government for taking the tract of land on which Fort Miles was built. In 1951 the State of Delaware as the owner in fee of the land, and having the power to dispose of the money it received from the government in any way its Courts or Legislature may see fit, chose to turn the sum over to the town of Lewes to provide a sewer for the Lewes Beach and cottages.

In 1970 Lewes was still requesting control of about three-quarters of a mile of ocean beach front. Delaware, however, wanted all of the land for itself and chose rather to give money than land to Lewes.

GENERAL MILES

General Nelson Appleton Miles was born in Westminster, Massachusetts, on August 8, 1839. Miles left his job as a clerk in Boston when the War Between the States broke out in September 1861 and entered the Union Army as a Lieutenant of Volunteer Infantry. He probably received his commission as a member of the National Guard.

He served with great distinction in the Peninsular Campaign in fact in almost all the battles of the Army of the Potomac. He fought at Fredericksburg, Antietam and Chancellorsville where he was wounded and incapacitated until 1864. He was a brigade commander in the Wilderness and Spotsylvania battles. For his meritorious conduct he was promoted to the rank of Brigadier General of Volunteers, one of the youngest generals of the war, commanding at the age of twenty-five years.

He fought at Petersburg and Cold Harbor in 1864-1865. At Sutherland Depot, a place near Petersburg, Miles' division of the 2d Corps captured two artillery pieces and took 600 Confederate prisoners. When the war ended he was in temporary command of an army corps of 26,000 men.

He did not leave the Army when the volunteer troops were mustered out in 1865 but joined the Regular Army. In 1866 he was made a Colonel of a regular infantry regiment. He became a Brigadier in 1880, a Major General in 1890, and in 1895 he became Commanding General of the United States Army.

General Miles became an Indian fighter in the West for seventeen years from 1869 to 1886. He had many dealings with the Indians, fighting the Cheyenne, Kiowa and Commanche on Thano Estacada in 1875 and the Sioux in Montana in 1876. He captured Chief Joseph, chief of the Nez Perces in 1877 in the Bare Paw Mountains of Northern Montana, and defeated the Chiricahua Apaches and the notorious Geronimo in 1886.

As a result of the political and military operations conducted by General Miles in 1891, the hostile expression of the Ghost Dance Cult among the Sioux were ended. The so-called Ghost Cult started among the Paiutes of Western Nevada as a religion. It spread rapidly among the Indians because of the feeling that the westward movement of white culture would destroy their native culture.

In 1890, administration changes in the United States Government and appointment of inexperienced men in charge of the reserves, along with broken pledges made to the Indians, especially among the Sioux, led to discontent and they set out to punish the white transgressors.

The Ghost Dance would begin in the late afternoon. Only individual dancers used musical instruments. A "ghost shirt," always made of white cloth and woven in Indian fashion, was worn by the dancers. It was also believed that by wearing the ghost shirt into battle it would protect the wearer from the white man's bullets. No metal was allowed to be worn. The leaders carried a ghost stick six feet long with red feathers and cloth. Other articles used were arrows, bow, sticks, and a gaming wheel. The ground would be consecrated and the priests ordained by the conferment of a consecrated feather from the sacred bird of the Ghost Dance Cult, the eagle. Sometimes a crow feather was used. The feathers were painted, as were the dancers, in elaborate designs of red, green, yellow and blue.

Participants fell into a trance that was designed to strengthen spiritual vision and physical health. Upon regaining consciousness, they narrated their visions. Any member who stayed away would be punished. All would then bathe to wash away any evil spirits. The general purpose of the dance, as an element of religion, was to focus the whole community's attention upon the message of salvation or Indian heaven.

Sioux leaders, Sitting Bull and Red Cloud, were the worst enemies of the whites, and much killing prevailed on both sides. Sitting Bull, a medicine man rather than a secular chief, was killed in December of 1890 and by January of 1891 the outbreak ended and a truce was signed at the Pine Ridge Agency in South Dakota.

There were many battles between the Indians and the troops under General Miles' command. The Sioux Wars started in 1854 and ended with the Messiah War from which the outgrowth of the Ghost Dance Cult originated.

In 1867 the Comanche, Kiowa and the Kataka Indians were put on a reservation in the Wichita Mountains in Western Oklahoma. The Arapaho and Cheyenne were also put on a reservation in the Western Oklahoma area.

The Indians again and again slipped away from their reservation to raid along the borders of Colorado, Kansas, New Mexico and Texas.

The troops under Miles, after more than fourteen battles, defeated the Indians encamped along the Red River and Canyons of the Staked Plains in the summer of 1874.

General Miles won wide acclaim for the way he handled the Germaine Girls incident. The Cheyenne had captured four of the girls on one of their raids, but two of them were recaptured in Texas in November of 1875. The two girls, five and seven years old and misused by the Indians, were sent to Fort Leavenworth Hospital for medical treatment and rest. The sisters reported of two more sisters still held captive by the Cheyenne.

Miles, outraged with the treatment of the little girls by the Cheyenne, sent a Kiowa scout to the tribe with a photograph of the two still held captive. He demanded the surrender of the girls and return of the tribe to the reservation or they would suffer complete annihilation. The order was obeyed without bloodshed.

The Sioux separated after the Custer Fight and Miles chased Sitting Bull into Canada in 1876. Sitting Bull, however, was able to evade Miles and slip back into the United States the next year.

Several years after the death of George Custer, at the battle of the Little Big Horn, a map taken from an Indian was brought to General Miles. Miles recognized it as (General) Lieutenant Colonel Custer's campaign map of the Black Hills of South Dakota and the Little Big Horn area of Montana. With the map was a message asking for reinforcements to come quickly. The text of the message was as follows:

> Benteen,
> Come on. Big village.
> Be quick. Bring packs.
>   W. W. Cooke
> P.S. Bring packs.

This message was written by the Regimental Adjutant, Lieutenant William W. Cooke. Custer sent his orderly, trumpeter Giovanni Martini, with the message to Captain Frederick W. Benteen, commander of one of the three columns into which Custer had divided the Seventh Cavalry Regiment.

Martini, his horse bleeding from a bullet wound, delivered the message to Benteen, who tried to reach Custer but was directed by Crow Scouts, whom Custer had detached earlier, to Reno's battalion. Benteen joined up with Major Reno, commander of another column, already engaged in combat, and the two columns were able to hold off the Indians until General Terry, expedition commander, arrived the next day to relieve them. Custer and his column were wiped out.

How the message fell into Indian hands is not known. It can only be surmised that it was lost or thrown on the battlefield, where it was picked up by the Indians as a war memento.

General Miles gave these papers to the widow of Colonel Custer who recognized them as a part of American History and gave them to the West Point Military Academy. This was where Colonel Custer received his commission as an officer in the United States Army. His remains were exhumed and reinterred at West Point in 1877.

General Miles defeated Crazy Horse at Wolf Mountain in 1877, and Big Foot surrendered to his overwhelming forces at the Wounded Knee Creek Battle. The battle was called an Indian massacre with 200 to 300 warriors killed and only 29 white troopers lost.

William F. (Buffalo Bill) Cody served as Army Chief of Scouts under General Miles and, in his World-Famous Wild West Show, reenacted the Indian surrender to General Miles at Pine Ridge.

After a year-long chase along the U.S.-Mexico border, the notorious Geronimo surrendered his small band of renegades to General Miles in the Chiricahua Mountain region of Arizona.

One of the reasons the Indians, especially the Apaches, held out for many years against the superior forces of the white soldiers was their remarkable knowledge of water holes and springs in their natural habitat.

Paintings on stones around the water holes and other indications showed they were highly valued as religious places as well as a water supply.

Miles established a system of putting guards on all known watering places and would attack the surprised Indians or drive them away from the water. This brought the Indians to final submission and they returned to the reservation.

Then in 1894 General Miles was put in command of the United States Troops sent to Chicago during the railway riots and Pullman strike of that year.

During the Spanish-American War in 1898 he directed military operations against Spain and was personally in command of the almost unopposed Puerto Rico expeditions. He was raised to the rank of Lieutenant General in 1900 and retired from active service in 1903.

General Miles died in Washington, D.C. on May 15, 1925, the end of a brilliant and gallant career of 42 years serving his country.

Why not immortalize General Miles by naming a great fort after him? He was Commanding General of the United States Army, a position alone worthy of the honor. But during the Civil War he commanded units in the Wilderness Campaign, Cold Harbor, Spotsylvania, Petersburg, Fredericksburg, Chancellorsville and Antietam. Wasn't the Delaware National Guard there also as the First Delaware Volunteers fighting as a unit of the Army of the Potomac?

During the Spanish American War, the First Delaware Infantry was ordered to join General Wade's division in Puerto Rico, under the command of General Miles. But their orders were changed and they were sent to Camp Meade. They almost came under the personally commanded expedition of General Miles in Puerto Rico.

General Miles fought Indians and there is evidence of Indians once living at Henlopen. He also was well acquainted with sand in his exploits of the West, and Fort Miles is a very sandy place. He also put down a Ghost uprising, and there is said to be a Ghost Ship legend at Henlopen. It is sometimes seen on a moonlit night when the water is calm and the wind just right, sailing into the Delaware Bay with the skull and crossbones flying from her mast. This is a story told around many a campfire at Henlopen.

All of these facts and legends are somewhat remote and are not necessarily related but do tend to make an interesting comparison as to how Fort Miles might have received its name.

General Miles wrote several books over the years during his career in the army. He wrote "Personal Recollections" in 1896, "Military Europe" in 1898, and "Observations Abroad" in 1899 and, after his retirement he wrote "Serving the Republic," in 1911. But as far as anyone can tell, he never set foot on Cape Henlopen. Just like the State of Delaware, named after a man who never set foot on Delaware soil or sailed on Delaware's waters, Fort Miles was named after a man who never saw the Great Dunes of Henlopen where the mighty Fort Miles was built.

SHIPS AND HENLOPEN

There are many stories of the ships that have sailed in and out of the mouth of the Delaware Bay. Some were to stay forever on the bay's floor.

Seventeenth century settlers and seamen were quick to see the importance of Henlopen as a whaling station. There were enough whales off the coast of Henlopen to lead the early Dutch to establish a town at the mouth of the Delaware Bay. No one knows how many whales were taken in the early days or when the whale population declined. But the Coast Guard and private fishing boats as well as commercial fishing fleet operators still report, generally in the winter, spouting whales from time to time.

Ancient whale bones, weighing as much as 400 pounds have been dredged up while deepening the channel at the Indian River Inlet. They can be seen at the Zwaanendael Museum in Lewes.

In March of 1638 a group of Swedes headed by Peter Minuit, a Dutchman, sailed past Cape Henlopen on the *Kalmar Nyckel* and landed at the rocks (Wilmington). They called their garrison "Christina Skants " (fort) in honor of their queen.

The *Kalmar Nyckel* set out on her return trip to Sweden in June of 1638 with a cargo of beaver and otter pelts and bearskins invoiced at 5917 florins or about $3,000. In 1640 she made a second voyage to Fort Christina. In 1648 she was reported too old to repair and no further record of her is known. On September 28, 1997, a replica was launched and she can be seen regularly in the summer docked in Lewes, Delaware, or along the Christina River in Wilmington.

William Penn, on his first voyage to America, sailed up the Delaware River past Cape Henlopen on the ship *Welcome* in 1682.

In 1780 Thomas Fisher, a lad of only seventeen, and one of his father's slaves were seized by a press gang and taken aboard the British frigate *Roebuck*, lying near Cape Henlopen, and held for ransom. Fisher's father was informed that he could redeem them for one hundred bullocks. The ransom was paid and they were released. Thomas Fisher later became sheriff of Sussex County and twice held that office.

There are other stories of ships and Cape Henlopen. There is the story of Betsy Patterson of Baltimore who married Jerome Bonaparte, the youngest brother of Napoleon Bonaparte. In 1804 they tried to sneak out of the United States to go to France. They got passage on the ship *Philadelphia*, a three-masted vessel leaving from Port Penn. It sailed down the Delaware River and ran aground in a storm and the passengers had to be rowed to the Henlopen Lighthouse and safety.

Shipwreckers were the cause of many wrecks in the waters near Cape Henlopen. A trick, generally associated with tales of England, was told of a small boy riding a donkey around a haystack on a dark stormy night and holding a lantern to simulate the Henlopen Light. This maneuver confused navigators of sailing ships and they would run aground. Their cargoes, or what was left, were retrieved by the waiting pirates. The long stretches of uninhabited marshes and beach were ideal for smugglers and pirates.

Pirates like Captain Canoot in 1698 anchored off Cape Henlopen and sacked the town of Lewes. Captain Kidd, a bloody buccaneer, is believed to have provisioned his ship from the Lewes chandlers. The Spanish privateer, Don Vincent Lopez, preyed on shipping in the area. James Gillam, believed to be from a pirate ship, was put ashore on Henlopen with several chests and another buried treasure legend emanated. Blueskin the pirate is another believed to have plundered the coast of Henlopen. Rumors and incidents of smuggling persisted for over a century after English warships drove most of the rogues out. But the pirates and smugglers reappeared in force during the Revolutionary War, and many a ship had to wait months under the protection of forts along the Delaware River for a chance to slip past the piratical crafts that preyed in the Delaware Bay.

The American Congress commissioned pirates themselves to put a stop to the raiders by hunting them down, but the pirateers did not disappear until after the American Civil War.

Known smugglers and contrabanders returned in 1940 and the Coast Guard was put on special lookout for them.

In 1889 the pilot boat *Enoch Turley*, a two-masted schooner, was lost in a hurricane off the Henlopen Cape. The S.S. *Lenape* caught fire and was beached on Cape Henlopen in 1925. The S.S. *Mohawk*, also in 1925, caught fire and broke in two and sank in the Delaware Bay. The *Long Island*, a fishing trawler owned by the Consolidated Fisheries Company of Lewes, went down in a gale in 1936 near Cape Henlopen.

During the Second World War a foreign freighter sailed into the Delaware Bay past Fort Miles on its way to one of the ports on the Delaware River. All ships were checked and provided with a pilot. This ship was ordered by radio to stop and wait for a boarding party. The ship did not answer and proceeded on. She was then signaled by flag and light to halt. The freighter continued on her way. Fort Miles fired her only shots in anger that day by firing two or three three-inch shots across the freighter's bow. The ship almost immediately became dead in the water. It was learned later that the ship had not seen the flag and light signals and her radio was not working. After inspection she was allowed to proceed on her way. That is how Fort Miles fired her only shots in defense of the Delaware Bay.

12-inch gun at Fort Miles by Henry L. Jacobs

Early in 1942 a sub-hunter fleet was started at the Milford Boatyard. Private as well as fishing boats were given depth charges to drop on any sub they might encounter. It was lucky these boats did not encounter any enemy subs, because they were not told by the Navy that they were too slow to get out of the way of the explosion of the depth charge after it was dropped overboard.

The German Submarine was more important than any other target. B-24 Bombers from Dover Army Air Base were sent to the Delaware Bay and Atlantic Ocean for sub patrol. Later the B-24s were sent to Florida and replaced by B-25s.

The Georgetown Naval Airfield at Georgetown, Delaware, however, was used only as a training base for fighter planes. The aircraft would make simulated aircraft carrier landings on the field. The Rehoboth airfield, a grass field started in 1938, was taken over by the Civil Air Patrol and directed sub-stalking activities from there in early 1942. The CAP used 300-pound depth charges and made several hits and sinkings on enemy subs.

U-boats sunk 472 ships in the Atlantic Ocean the first half of 1942. The tender *John R. Williams* hit a mine and sank at the mouth of the Delaware Bay on June 11, 1949. A German sub, the U-373, commanded by Oberlieutenant Zur See Loser came with the express purpose of closing the Delaware Bay. The sub's Captain set up a barrier of naval mines off the Delaware Coast by discharging the mines through the torpedo tubes. The mines, G.S. Type, and over 2,000 lbs., looked like a torpedo except both ends were blunt. They were 8' 6" long when discharged but were extended to 15' 5" when the detonators were extended. The Bay was closed to shipping for four days before mine sweepers could clear the bay entrance.

German U-boats were sunk off the coast of Henlopen during the Second World War. Mute testimony were the oil slicks and clothing washed ashore on Henlopen. When Germany surrendered on May 6 at 9:41 p.m. Eastern Standard Time, Admiral Doenitz, who thought his U-boat fleet would rule the sea and win the war, assumed the scepter from Hitler. Upon his command, most U-boats surfaced and raised the white flag of surrender. The U-805, one of the first to surrender, surfaced off the Delaware Bay early in the morning of May 9, 1945. It was taken in tow and hauled to Fort Miles for examination before hauling to Philadelphia as a prize. Later it was put on display for the public at different ports along the Delaware River. A second German sub, the U-858, was put on display at the Fort's pier on November 22, 1945.

Conditions for U-boats surrendering were to cut their deck guns off and dump them overboard, along with all other weapons and explosives, and to cut a hole in the side of the conning tower so the sub would be unable to submerge. Prisoners were also kept on board for a time in case any time bombs had been set. More than 400 U-boats surrendered along the Atlantic Coast and some time after the war they were all sunk in the Atlantic off the coast of Maine.

Even during the World War in 1918 German submarines appeared off the coast of Henlopen, and a mine near Cape Henlopen sank the tanker *Herbert L. Pratt* that same year.

All kinds of ships have passed through the Delaware Bay past Cape Henlopen and old Fort Miles including the largest aircraft carrier built in the Delaware Valley, the *Kitty Hawk*, and also the only active battleship in the world in 1969, the *New Jersey*, a World War II battle wagon brought back from mothballs to fight in the South China Sea in the Vietnam War.

During the late eighteenth century, Great Britain, France, and Spain became locked in a military struggle of a global scale known as the War with Revolutionary France and the Napoleonic Wars. The armies and navies of these warring powers became engaged on

U-858 before being towed to the 4th Naval District, Philadelphia
(Delaware in Wolrd War II Collection. Courtesy of the Delaware Public Archives)

every continent, and nearly every sea around the world. Critical to these countries' military success was the maintenance of their own, or the destruction of their adversaries overseas markets. The young United States provided an important outlet for British manufactured goods. As the 1790s progressed, the British government sought to protect its American markets from French commerce raiders and military vessels by having the merchant convoys to North America escorted by ships of the Royal Navy.

After having been engaged in this duty, HMB *DeBraak* capsized and sank in a sudden squall off the Delaware coast on May 25, 1798. The vessel's captain, Commander James Drew, and about one-half of the ship's company perished in the sinking. The brig settled in about eighty feet of water, and over nearly two centuries gradually became part of the archeological record and maritime lore of the Atlantic coast.

The *DeBraak* and its associated collection of 20,000 artifacts presents an unparalleled look into the naval life in the heyday of the Royal Navy, and important clues to a better understanding of the human experience at sea. This rich and diverse collection includes the surviving hull remnant and the many artifacts represent every facet of shipboard life. The hull, of which thirty-percent survives, is the only known example of the architecture of a class of vessels called the brig-sloop.

These small but powerful vessels would see expanded and important service throughout the above periods. Many of the artifacts, such as footwear and small arms collection, are the largest ones known from a naval context. Many others are remarkably rare, such as a group of eight canister, giant shotgun-like projectiles capable of inflicting casualties in an enemy ship's crew, which are still packed in their original box. Ship fittings, rigging components, made by Walter Taylor of Southampton, England, a new type of cannon called a carronade and flintlock gunlocks to fire them, bear witness to important technological innovations that revolutionized the production of ship's fittings, facilitated tactical changes, and expanded British seapower. This innovation can also be seen in the application of carronades, which were a new type of cannon designed to fire a heavy projectile, but at the same time were intended to reduce the enormous weights carried aboard ships. These guns tripled the *DeBraak's* firepower while reducing the weight carried by the vessel by nearly two tons.

Navigational instruments, a sailmaker's palm, and the surgeons bone saw and tooth key reveal the many skills, training and expertise required to keep a small vessel functioning at sea. Ceramic plates, table glass, uniform coat buttons, furniture fragments and a silver trophy cup, a perpetual calendar for the year 1798, one of the cubes from the game of chance called crown and anchor, and a narrowing ring used by Captain Drew in memory of his brother and nephew, who had drowned earlier in the year, are just but a few of the artifacts that reveal the many facets of the human dimensions of life at sea and social interaction among the ship's company. Interestingly, many of the ceramic plates were used by the common sailors, and indicate they enjoyed an improved level of material culture over that used earlier by sailors in the Royal Navy.

Over the past fourteen years, the State of Delaware has provided nearly 1.5 million dollars that has supported the work of professional archeologists, historians, material culture specialists, and conservators. Much of this work is still ongoing. Current activities are also being directed at the preservation of the surviving hull remnant and the many iron artifacts such as the cannon, shot, ballast, and anchors. These efforts, as well as the commitment to long-term curation, will ensure the survival of the *DeBraak* collection well into the 21st century.

To build the breakwater in 1825 trees were cut from atop the Henlopen dunes, removing the cover that kept the sand in place. The sand shifted freely in the wind and thus the coastline moved inland and eventually toppled the old Henlopen Light House, nicknamed "Old Man of the Sea."

In 1883 the *Minnie Hunter* hit Hen and Chicken Shoal, which lies just under the water off the end tip of the cape, and went aground. The wreck became a jetty and the erosion process was slowed temporarily. The shoreline was changed and the tip of the cape extended itself further into the bay making it somewhat closer to the wreck of the *De Braak*.

The currents of the Delaware Bay circle around toward the beach and flow north again assisting the wave motion which pushes the sand along the beach instead of washing over it. This motion extends the cape along into the bay. The movement, however, is very slow but determines how the cape tip grows while the coastline recedes. The coastline, however, moves more rapidly, at a rate of 12 feet or more a year.

A black sand, sometimes mistaken for oil, is deposited on the Delaware Bay shore. The sand is ilmenite ore used in the manufacturing of paint and titanium metal. Although the ore has a high percentage of titanium dioxide, the deposit is too small to recover, but indicates there is a large deposit somewhere in the Delaware Bay, between Mispillion Light and Lewes.

Dozens of once proud ships lie entombed beneath the sand and the water of the Delaware Bay. Fishermen hook their lines on them or anchors from their boats scrape across these long-forgotten vessels. Sometimes pieces of wood and metal wash ashore, but the sea and wind soon bury them again.

The Delaware Valley has been the center of shipbuilding in America since the time of William Penn. Shipyards along the Delaware River were Dravo, Harlan and Hollingsworth, and Pusey and Jones in Wilmington, and Sun Ship, Hog Island Shipyard, New York Ship, William Cramp and Sons Shipbuilding, Mathias

Marine Exchange Tower, 1968
(Courtesy of C. W. Warrington)

and Company, and the famous Philadelphia Naval Shipyard that built the largest ship ever built in the Valley in 1943, the famous battleship the U.S.S. *New Jersey*. The U.S.S. *Pennsylvania*, a product of the original Philadelphia Navy Yard in 1827, a ship of the line, was the largest sailing vessel ever built for the Navy. The first ship built for the U.S. Navy, in 1776, by Wharton and Humphreys, was the frigate *Randolph*.

In 1844 the *Bangor* was the first sea-going Iron propeller steamer built in America, and she was built in Wilmington. The first vessel to fly the American flag in a foreign port was the brig *Nancy*, also built in Wilmington.

Many, many ships were built on the Delaware—armed steamers, ironclad frigates, and ocean liners like the S.S. *St. Paul* in 1894 and the S.S. *Washington* in 1933. Protected cruisers and light cruisers, oilers and cargo ships were built in vast numbers. The aircraft carrier *Saratoga* was built in the Valley in 1927 and so were the battleships *Utah* in 1911 and the famed "Battleship X", the *South Dakota* in 1941.

The battleship Utah, over 30 years old, was being used as a target ship in 1941 at Pearl Harbor when it was hit by warplanes from Japan and rendered useless.

Is it any wonder the United States Government built a mighty fort like Miles to protect one of the oldest and largest ship-building basins in North America, the Delaware Valley?

Convoys, which formed off the Delaware coast, were protected by the big guns of this fort from surface craft and air attacks.

Men stationed at the fort could sometimes see the fires of ships, torpedoed not far from the Delaware Coast by the hit and run tactics of the German U-Sub Wolf Packs.

Governor's Day at National Guard Camp, Fort Miles. Gov. Carvel,
top right and Lt. Gov. Bayard, right, third from top.
(General Collection: Military.
Courtesy of the Delaware Public Archives)

This was not the first time people watched ships under attack off the Delaware Coast. In the days when piracy thrived off the Henlopen Cape residents of Lewes would watch pirates prey on ships flying the flags of Spain and France. They found it great sport and would hike to the 80-foot Big Dune with the whole family for a picnic outing.

The Cape May-Lewes Ferry now plies between Lewes, Delaware, and Cape May, New Jersey, across the mouth of the Delaware Bay. The entrance to the ferry on the Delaware side is near the entrance to Henlopen State Park.

It is said that Henlopen was named for a Dutch town, but some historians say that when Cornelius May sailed into the bay he gave his name to the north shore and the name of a friend and financial backer, Thymen Jacobson Hinlopen, to the south shore. Hence Cape May, New Jersey, and Cape Henlopen, Delaware.

The trip across the bay takes a little less than 70 minutes and is about 16.3 miles. Launched in July 1964, the ferry is a direct route or short cut to the Chesapeake Bay Bridge-Tunnel traveling south, or if going north a short cut to the South Jersey sea resorts.

But this was not the first ferry to travel from Cape May to Lewes. Sidewheel steamers took tourists across the bay around 1900.

Some excursions were from Philadelphia and Wilmington down the Delaware River to the Bay. Another excursion was from the Port of Baltimore on a steamer down the Chesapeake Bay about 20 miles and across to Love Point, opposite Annapolis. Then they would board a train and ride across the Delaware-Maryland Peninsula to Lewes. At Lewes they would cross the Delaware Bay on another steamer and disembark at Cape May Point. After a pleasant day at the beach and dinner of seafood at Cape May or Lewes, the tourists would return to their home port.

Photo of gun battery 519 at Fort Miles
(Courtesy of Tom Maier, from Wisconsin,
stationed at Fort Miles for 2½ years)

Even in Alaska there is a Cape Henlopen. It is in the form of a U.S. Coast Guard Cutter, a 95-foot patrol boat, built in Curtis Bay, Maryland, in 1958.

The *Cape Henlopen's* duties are search and rescue work and aids in navigation. Since the area in southeast Alaska is a national forest and virtually unpopulated, the only means of transportation is by boat and seaplanes. Fishermen, hunters, and pleasure boats are attracted to this Pacific Rain Forest where the famed brown bear roams, and seal, deer, goats, ducks and geese are plentiful. Most game is found on numerous islands in the area and boats are necessary. The *Cape Henlopen* is kept busy in the Tongass National Forest in this naturalists' paradise, about as far as one can get in the southern part of Alaska and still remain in the United States.

The most important fish in the United States is not eaten but is used primarily for oil and fertilizer. It is called the menhaden, and there was a large processing plant on Cape Henlopen that operated when the fish were running.

The menhaden used to abound in Delaware waters and the Atlantic Ocean. The young fish would use the rivers and bays and the adjoining marshes as a nursery ground, but there are few around now, probably because of pollution.

Military personnel newly stationed at Miles in the 1940s and 50s were sometimes sickened by the foul smell of the Henlopen Fish Factory. Fortunately it did not last for more than a couple of days at a time.

Fishing fleets would unload their catch at the processing plant and sail out again for more fish. The boats would sometimes be out for a week or more.

Ships come and go past Cape Henlopen and the old "Masked Fortress" so called because her big 16-inch guns with barrels 55 feet long were once buried deep underground. But, although the big guns are gone from the cape, the cape will be there long after the last ship has disappeared.

First discharges leaving Fort Miles, Oct. 15, 1945
(Delaware in World War II Collection.
Courtesy of the Delaware Public Archives)

CAPE HENLOPEN STATE PARK

Delaware, at a ceremony on October 17, 1964, at 11 A.M., took transfer of the property formerly known as Fort Miles from the Department of the Army. Political leaders, including the Delaware General Assembly and the Delaware Congressional Delegation, the Secretary of the Army, Secretary of the Interior, conservation groups and civic leaders were present at the ceremony. The Delaware Congressional Delegation was instrumental in getting the transfer of the land through Congress.

The acreage turned over to the state was a little over 554 acres. The state, however, handed over a check for $61,000 to reimburse the federal government for what it paid for the land when it was obtained for defense purposes from Delaware.

The State sold some of the buildings and they were moved off the parkland. Some of the other buildings, like the cement block barracks and latrines were torn down and the two-story barracks and some mess halls were burned down to reduce maintenance costs.

The Inshore Underwater Warfare Division, U.S. Naval Reserve remained, in an old bunker, 60 by 150 feet and 40 feet high. The bunker formerly held 6-inch guns of the old Coastal Defense Artillery units.

The reserve unit was mainly concerned with underwater detection. Its mission is to control the seaward approaches to the Delaware Bay by detecting submarine defense and activity in shallow water areas.

Sonar buoys, radar and sonar equipment are used to detect objects. Their mission is to "detect, define and destroy." The division continues to hold reserve meetings and guard the Delaware Bay entrance.

126

The section dubbed the "100" area by state park officials is a tract of land in the heart of Cape Henlopen which has been maintained by the Air Force before and after the land was made a parkland. It is used by the Dover Air Base as a recreation area for its personnel. The Air Force, however, owns and maintains most of the existing structures and is entitled to use any of the facilities until the state should decide to develop the area for other purposes, such as a bathhouse or parking lot or some other recreational type facility for the public.

The Air Force puts a very sizeable investment into the area each year and, although they hold no lease with the Park Commission, they run a responsible beach facility and keep the place looking good in appearance.

The National Guard could have had all of the property formerly known as Fort Miles turned over to them as a state military base and received financial help from the government to maintain it. But due to political influence and the decision of state military leaders, they decided to utilize the Bethany Beach Reservation as a state training establishment, to the dismay of many guardsmen and citizens alike. State Archives are now housed in the underground bunkers once used for the big guns.

The National Guard used the ammo bunkers in back of the family campgrounds to store its ammo for training purposes. Although the guard did not fire at Miles, it did fire its air defense guns during summer camps at the nearby Bethany Beach Army Reservation. The Navy station at the fort also used some of the bunkers for ammo and other supplies. The now empty bunkers with their heavy steel doors would make an ideal air raid shelter for people living in the area.

In 1965 the Federal Government transferred a 10½ acre tract of land in Lewes, formerly occupied by the Army Hospital for Fort Miles, to the Lewes School Board, which erected a new elementary school on the site.

The auxiliary water supply for the old army post hospital, a well and pumping station and a 100,000-gallon storage tank on three-tenths of an acre of land were also turned over to the Lewes Board of Public Works in October of the same year, to be used as a possible standby reserve for the town.

In 1969 the Delaware National Guard became a signal unit and turned in the last of a long history of artillery pieces. The end of artillery firing practice at the Bethany Reservation was over, unless the Federal Government was to bring in reserve units from other states.

The 1st Army has a recreation area near the naval facility. They used old restored one-story cement block barracks on a high sand dune overlooking the ocean in the southern part of the old post.

Cape Henlopen is one of Delaware's finest parks. There are many outdoor recreation facilities on the cape: ocean bathing, camping, hiking, surf fishing, and picnicking. Tables and grills are available as well as drinking water and sanitary facilities. A bathhouse is also available with cold-water showers.

Even beach buggies, with valid permits, are permitted in the Gordon Pond Area, north of the old Army observation tower to the Navy property line.

There is an organized youth-group camp program at Henlopen. It allows for children camping under the direct supervision of adult leaders who are responsible for their conduct and safety. There are also resident youth-group camps, which allow children to occupy buildings, and other facilities provided by the Park Commission under the direct supervision of adult leaders.

These groups do not include family groups. Family groups must camp in the family camping area with a single piece of transportation and equipment that will provide privacy, such as a camper truck.

A youth group must consist of youths affiliated with scouts, schools, churches, clubs or similar type organizations. There are both girl and boy groups. These camp groups are permitted to use the old Fort Miles facilities for a small fee. Included are the barracks, now called dormitories, game courts, a gymnasium, chapel, mess halls, and of course, the sanitary facilities. Cots and mattresses are furnished. The State Park for the safety and protection of the public employs lifeguards.

Other programs for the public, provided under the supervision of the Delaware Nature Education Center and State Park Commission of Delaware, is two nature trails: the Seaside Trail and the Pinelands Trail.

Cape Henlopen State Park has a naturalist, and guided trail tours are conducted there in the summer. There is also a nice little nature display at the visitor center, with specimens pertaining to the cape. There is a small bird sanctuary on the Henlopen Point beyond the square Maritime Exchange Tower, and many birds such as Piping Plover, Terns and Skimmers nest there. Other birds like gulls, several species, and sanderlings are found scurrying around looking for small fish and eels.

Living fossils, unchanged for 250 million years, are found on the Henlopen beach. The horseshoe crab or pan crab or swordtail, the name depending on the locality, comes between May and July each year, all along the Atlantic Coast, to spawn. The females, nearly half again as large as the males, climb up the beach to lay their eggs, with several males clinging on behind. The female pauses every few feet to scoop a hole in the sand and as many as a thousand greenish eggs the size of buckshot are deposited. The male scatters his sperm over them, and the dragging bodies cover the eggs with sand. As many as 20,000 eggs may be laid by one horseshoe crab. All of these eggs do not survive, some are laid too close to the water's edge, others too far ashore. Still, fish and eels gobble others up. Shore birds take their toll as well. Early Indians living on the dunes watched where the birds were feeding and took the eggs to eat like caviar.

Hundreds of thousands of the crabs were taken in the twenties and thirties and fed to pigs or were used for fertilizer by farmers in Sussex County. Fishermen sometimes use the crab shells for bailing out their boats. They cut the crabmeat up for eel bait.

Some states, such as Massachusetts, have a bounty of four cents each for living crabs because they can wreak havoc among shellfish, especially soft-shelled clams buried in mud flats where horseshoe crabs hide and search for worms and mollusks to eat.

The horseshoe crab and the shellfish have lived together for millions of years. It is man who is spewing raw waste into the water of our Atlantic Coast and killing the kelp beds that produce oxygen. He is also poisoning the shellfish out of existence and quite possibly the horseshoe crab as well. Where there were once hundreds of thousands spawning on the Delaware beaches there are now tens of thousands.

The horseshoe, sometimes mistakenly called a king crab, is no longer used as a fertilizer. But the state is missing out on a great opportunity to make a little profit and create employment during the spring and summer by not picking up the dying horseshoe crabs, grinding and processing them in the seldom used fish factory at Lewes and making them into powder fertilizer to sell. The project would also be welcomed by the residents along the bay to be rid of the stench that occurs as the horseshoe decays on the beaches. The decaying horseshoe crab is also a breeding place for flies and could be one of the reasons so many flies are found on the beach.

The construction of Fort Miles did not destroy the so-called living sand, for the insects and animals are still there. The deer, fox and numerous cottontail rabbits still abound in the area. There are many different little funnel-like depressions in the sand, made by the ants and ant lions, and chimney-like open holes of the wolf spiders. The saltmarsh mosquitoes and greenhead flies are still there in abundance. The pine lizard and the hognose snakes (puffadder) can still be seen by a sharp eye. The little Fowler's toad is eaten by the hognose snake and the toad eats the ants and flies, a never-ending cycle of nature.

The little hognose will scare the life out of you by hissing and spreading its neck like a cobra. It will not strike, but it coils up like it is going to strike and can scare an intruder away. If this does not work the snake will sometimes play dead and can be picked up without moving.

The old bunkers were camouflaged during the Second World War to hide the fort from the air. Plantings made to hide the sandhill structures were bush honeysuckle, trumpet creeper, bittersweet, black locust and red cedar.

131

Top of a bunker at Fort Miles as it appears today
(Courtesy of Delaware Division of Parks and Recreation, Cultural
Resources and Recreational Services Section.)

All kinds of berries are there, like the waxy bayberries that are eaten by the birds. Early settlers made candles from the bayberries. The famous wild cranberry bogs are still there, and the beach plums are still found. Blackberries as well as wild cherry and sassafras trees are the birds' paradise. Wrens, woodpeckers, tree swallows, sparrows and grackles, birds of all kinds visit Henlopen.

Poison plants like sumac and ivy are found there. Trees of all kinds-willow, poplar, pine, and vines like the Virginia creeper, plants like low beach heather and grasses, all help hold the sand dunes together by breaking the forces of the wind and anchor the sand with their roots.

The prickly pear cactus is also present and in the wetter spots is found marsh and royal ferns, sphagnum moss and red maples. All of these and more can be found at Cape Henlopen State Park.

The University of Delaware has a marine biology laboratory at Henlopen. Classes are held in a former warehouse of the old fort and the old post headquarters is now used as an office for the laboratory. The university obtained a lease from the state in 1966 on 14 acres for research around Delaware's salt marshes and shallow bays. The marine laboratory now has a 40-foot ketch, the *Wolverine*, for checking oyster beds and surveying fish Population and other marine studies.

Some of the research projects include trying to isolate the cause of a disease devastating the Delaware Bay oysters and contaminating the clams. It was found that a single-cell microscopic organism was causing the disease but how to control it was another matter. Attempts are being made to develop a disease-resistant strain of oyster. Another study, of the sand tubeworm, which builds on any hard base to form a rock-hard castle-like structure in the sand, might provide a way to combat shore erosion.

Headquarters at Fort Miles by Henry L. Jacobs. The building still stands today.

Marine biology has expanded rapidly at the university and will continue to expand in the future. The marine laboratory is a great asset for the waters of Delaware Bay and the great salt marshes.

There was a "save the dunes" fight that started in 1967 for those dunes not in the Henlopen State Park. The dunes and the Lewes trash dump greet arrivals coming into Delaware from the Lewes-Cape May Ferry. Sand has been trucked away, and construction of a new plant near the State Park entrance (Barcroft Co.) has begun to advance on the historically significant and picturesque dunes. The State Department sought legislation that might bring the dunes under their jurisdiction and preserve them. However, the town of Lewes has apparent jurisdiction over the land with titles dating back to the William Penn grant. Lewes tried to help, by revision of a long-term lease with one firm, which had been removing sand and by seeking a new place to dump their trash. By 1971, shifting sand and new shrubs had all but covered the dump.

Fort Miles was not a retired fort just because the State of Delaware had made a public park out of part of it. Fort Miles was still an active military installation as late as 1971. The Navy was there in the southern part of the dunes on the oceanfront. Three large, circular radio towers marked their location.

Again, as in 1940, when the Army was so secret about building a harbor defense system, the Navy kept its secret about what its mission was at Fort Miles. There was much speculation as to what the government was doing inside the sand dunes. The Navy patrolled the area and would not let anyone near the installations without proper clearance.

There were rumors as to what the government was doing. One held that the facility was an emergency White House communications center in case of a national emergency. The President and top government personnel could be flown the relatively short distance to Fort Miles from Washington D.C. and

Concrete Coast Watch and Control Tower by Henry L. Jacobs

set up a command center or secret war room. It could also be a place to rush high government and military officials in the time of an emergency and sneak them off to some other part of the world in a submarine.

But, again as in the past, the government in 1970 announced that it would shut down the Navy's radio station at Miles as part of a nationwide program to cut defense costs.

Senator John J. Williams of Delaware started procedures and inquiries at the General Services Administration to convert the radio station property into parkland.

Under normal procedure the General Services Administration would be charged with the disposal of excess government property. The disposal would take many months because all other branches of the services would have to be asked, and each branch would have to decide if the radio station would be of any use to them. However, if the Defense Department declared the property surplus, it would be transferred to the General Services Administration which would auction it to the highest bidder. In 1964 this procedure had been circumvented through legislation introduced by Williams.

In 1970 the Army began bulldozing part of the Great Sand Hill to make a flat area for Army personnel camping during their summer vacation.

This move upset citizens of Lewes and Delaware leaders. Delaware congressmen said the land was not needed for Army recreation, but they would like to have it as a public park for the people of Delaware. They also said the Army was destroying the natural beauty of the dunes. Many people visited the areas soon after the leveling of the dunes and could not see where the Army had destroyed it whatsoever.

The dunes of Cape Henlopen State Park
(Photo by Jack Goins, Delaware Division of State Parks and
Recreation, Cultural Resources and Recreational Services Section)

The people who complained so much about the Army upsetting the ecology and natural beauty of the dunes seemed to forget that in 1941 the Army bulldozed many acres to construct Fort Miles. If the ecology or natural beauty were ruined it would have been ruined then. But the Army in 1941 as well as in 1970 stabilized the property around the great dunes with topsoil and plantings of several kinds and therefore didn't destroy it at all.

The armed services need and depend on low-cost vacations for their personnel and try to make their lives more pleasant by providing recreational facilities for them. The military have been at Henlopen in some form or another since 1873 and have the right to do whatever they think best for national defense, and to make a military family happy by providing an economical recreational area for them is in the interest of national defense.

In May of 1970 Senators J. Caleb Boggs and John J. Williams co-sponsored a bill that stipulated that the land at Henlopen revert to the state at the original cost to the federal government and to have the remaining Army property and adjoining land held by the Navy transferred to the State of Delaware for use as a park. The legislation forbids disposal of the land by the state for commercial use. The legislation completed the park development at Henlopen, started in 1964 when the State of Delaware obtained title to over 500 acres, converted from the Army's Fort Miles Base.

The Navy, in the winter of 1971, surrendered 256 acres to the General Services Administration for disposal. A parcel of 240 acres inland from their oceanographic laboratory center and 16 acres of small holdings scattered throughout the Cape Henlopen Park area made up the acres surrendered.

A connecting road, under consideration for a long time, was now possible between Cape Henlopen State Park and other state-owned lands north of Rehoboth Beach. This corridor would allow a road to be built on solid ground. A road could have been built before the acquisition of the Navy lands, on state property at Whiskey Beach in the south but would have gone through marshland. The Army's remaining tract totaled about 190 acres and they verbally relinquished that property in March of 1971.

The Army was allowed an area for maneuvers of its two giant LARC amphibious vehicles. Arrangements were also made for Army personnel, who use the tract as a vacation spot, to camp in the vicinity of their old recreational area. The Navy also kept its oceanographic center, an isolated 2-acre plot, for reserve training.

A mighty fort called Miles, after a long, hard fight to survive, finally surrendered to legislation and changing times, rather than to hostile military action.

The park continues to grow, additions coming from surplus government land, purchases and donations totaling more than 5,000 acres. Many of the buildings from the Fort Miles era have been preserved and adapted for park use, including the nature center which at one time was the Guard House for the fort.

Cape Henlopen State Park is the first park with open beaches that welcomes both swimmers and surf fisherman. The park provides habitat and protection for endangered Piping Plovers, and is a very popular destination for family camping.

APPENDICES

U-858 POWs in the chow line at Fort Miles
(Delaware in World War II Collection,
Courtesy of the Delaware Public Archives)

APPENDIX A

WAR DEPARTMENT,
OFFICE OF THE CHIEF OF ENGINEERS,
WASHINGTON

June 12, 1917

From: The Chief of Engineers

To: The Secretary of War.

Subject: Cession of Jurisdiction.

1. Negotiations are now in progress for the acquisition of certain land in the vicinity of the mouth of the Mispillion River, in Cedar Creek Hundred, Sussex County, Delaware, for use as a site for fortifications. The purchase of this property has heretofore been authorized by the Secretary of War.

2. The land to be acquired is more particularly described as follows:
"All that certain farm, tract, piece or parcel of land and premises, situated, lying and being in Cedar Creek Hundred, Sussex County and State of Delaware, on both sides of the public road, leading from Milford to Cedar Beach; bounded on the North by lands formerly of Trusten P. McCauley, deceased, and now of the said Angelina Marshall, on the East by lands formerly of the said Trusten P. McCaulley, deceased, and now of the said Angelina Marshall, and by Cedar Creek Canal, on the South by lands late of David Mills, deceased, and lands formerly of Elias Shockley, and now of Mark H. Shockley, known as the 'John C. Blackland,' on the West by lands late of Elias Shockley, and now of Mark H. Shockley, known as the 'John C. Black lands,' and by lands formerly of Curtis S. Watson, and now of Annie E. Watson, known as the 'Walton Farm.' The metes and bounds, courses and

143

distances, according to a survey thereof, made in the Month of May, AD 1917 by John C. Hopkins of Dover, Delaware, are as follows, to-wit-:

Beginning at a stake standing South nineteen and three quarters degrees (19 ¾) West two (2) feet from a stump of an old line white-oak tree, noted by all the old surveys; said stake stands near the West side of the said public road, and is in the line of lands of Annie E. Watson, a corner for this land and for lands of Mark H. Shockley. It being the original beginning corner for the lands hereby conveyed; thence running with the line of lands of the said Annie E. Watson, formerly known as the 'Walton Farm' North nineteen and three quarters (19¾) degrees East eighty-one and two-tenths (81 2/10) perches to the remains of a corner fence post in a soft marsh; being in line of lands of the said Annie E. Watson, and a corner for lands formerly of Trusten P. McCauley, deceased, and now of Angelina Marshall South eighty-four (84) degrees East twenty and six-tenths (20 6/10) perches to a post; thence South thirty-three degrees (33) East eleven and one-tenth (11 1/10) perches to a stake; thence South seventy-one and one-half (71 1/20) degrees East seventeen and seven tenths (17 7/10) perches to a large corner post in the angle of a division fence; thence running between two parallel banks South twenty-nine (29) degrees West twenty-five (25) perches to another post; thence running with the West side of another bank South thirty-eight and one-half degrees (38½) East nine and six-tenths (9 6/10) perches to a corner in the middle of the aforesaid public road, a line stake is set on the West side of said road; thence continuing with lands of the said Angelina Marshall along with the middle of the said public road North sixty-nine and one-half (69 ½) degrees East ten (10) perches to an angle therein; thence South seventy-six and one-quarter (76¼) degrees East one hundred and four (104) perches to another angle in the middle of said road, opposite the mouth of the public road leading to the lighthouse; thence continuing with the middle of the said public road, first mentioned, South sixty-four and one-half (64½) degrees East sixty-one and one-tenth (61 1/10) perches to a bolt-head in or near the middle of the said public road, at the West end of the iron draw-bridge, over Cedar Creek Canal (said bolt-head was pointed out as a bench mark, noted by the United States Engineer); thence running with the West edge of the said Cedar Creek Canal South twenty-eight (28) degrees West thirty (30) perches to an angle of said canal, at the end of a high bank; thence continuing with the West edge of said Canal South seventeen and one-quarter (17¼) degrees West one hundred and fifty-nine and four-tenths (159 4/10) perches to a corner on the West edge of said canal, at the North edge, and at the mouth of Black's Ditch; then leaving said canal, and running through the marsh North sixty-four and three-quarters (64 ¾) degrees West forty-seven and five-tenths (47 5/10) perches to a stake set on the soft marsh, at a corner for this land, land late of David Mills, deceased, and for lands of the said Mark H. Shockley; thence running with lands of the said Mark H. Shockley, formerly known as the "John C. Black land," North ten (10) 3 - degrees East forty-eight (48) perches to a stake on the marsh; thence North nine (9) degrees West fifty-six and twenty-five one-hundredths (56 25/100) perches to a stake on high land, under a division fence; then North fifty-nine and three-quarters (59¾) degrees West one-hundred and forty-five (145) perches to the place of beginning, and containing one hundred and fifty-one acres and twenty square perches (151 A. & 20 sq. p.) of upland and marsh, be the same more or less.

3. In view of the provisions of R. S. 355, it is recommended that this paper be referred to the Judge Advocate General with a view to the preparation of a draft of an act ceding to the United States jurisdiction over the land to be acquired, and that the matter be then presented to the Governor of the State of Delaware with request that he recommend to the legislature of that State the passage of the desired legislation at its next session. This action is requested in view of the fact that the land to be acquired consists of approximately151 acres while the general act of cession by the State of Delaware (Approved May 19, 1898-Laws of Delaware,

1898, p 3) applies only in cases where the land to be acquired does not exceed one hundred acres in area.

4. It is contemplated that an additional tract of land adjacent to the area described above will also be acquired, and proceedings in condemnation are about to be instituted for the acquisition of this land. While the exact area of this additional tract has not as yet been determined, and it is not possible at present to furnish an accurate description thereof, it is believed desirable that cession of jurisdiction therein by the State of Delaware be secured at this time, and it is accordingly recommended that the Judge Advocate General include in the draft of an act of cession, covering the area above described, a proviso covering the cession by the State of Delaware of jurisdiction in such additional adjacent land, not to exceed 200 acres, as may hereafter be acquired by the United States.

H. C. Newcomer
Colonel, Corps of Engineers.
Acting Chief of Engineers.

APPENDIX B

ADDRESS REPLY TO
"THE ATTORNEY GENERAL"
AND REFER TO
INITIALS AND NUMBER

186076-6

DEPARTMENT OF JUSTICE.
WASHINGTON, D.C.

OSL-AQ

June 14, 1917

JUN 18 1917

M. AND R. DIV. WAR DEPT.
601
JUN 15 1917
RECEIVED

The Secretary of War.

Sir:

I have the honor to refer to your letter of
May 24, 1917, requesting the acquisition, by condemnation,
of a parcel of land near the mouth of Mispillion River,
Delaware, for fortifications, in which you request that
such proceedings be instituted under authority of the Fortification Act approved August 18, 1890. In letter dated
June 12, 1917, from the United States Attorney it is suggested that proceedings be brought under the authority
contained in the Act of August 1, 1888 (25 Stat. 357),
for the reason that the law relating to condemnation in
force in the State of Delaware is in unsatisfactory condition.

I therefore suggest that your request for condemnation be redrafted and that reference to the Act of August
18, 1890, be omitted therefrom.

Respectfully,

For the Attorney General,

Assistant, Attorney General.

ASSISTANT AND CHIEF CLERK
JUN 15 1917
2 WAR DEPT.

JUN 22 1917

Memorandum from Attorney General's Office to Secretary of War
stating condemnation proceedings.

147

APPENDIX C

June 20, 1917

Honorable John G. Townsend, Jr.,
Governor of Delaware,
Dover, Delaware

Sir:

I beg to invite your attention to the fact that negotiations are now in progress for the purchase by the government for fortification purposes, of a tract of land containing 151 acres and 20 square perches in the vicinity of the mouth of the Mispillion River, in Cedar Creek Hundred Sussex County, Delaware, and also that it is proposed to acquire through condemnation proceedings an additional tract adjacent thereto for the said purposes the exact area of which has not yet been determined.

It is contemplated by Clause 17, Section 8, article 1 of the Constitution of the United States, that the government shall possess exclusive jurisdiction over all lands purchased within the limits of any state for fortification purposes, and by Section 355 of the Revised Statutes, it is provided that no public money shall be expended upon any site or land purchased for such purposes until the consent of the Legislature of the state in which the same is situated shall have been given to such purchase; or, in other words, until exclusive jurisdiction over such site or land shall have been ceded to the United States.

In view of the said provision of the Constitution and the requirements of Section 355 of the Revised Statutes, I have prepared and enclose herewith a draft of an Act granting the consent of the Legislature of the State of Delaware to the acquisition of the said tracts, and ceding jurisdiction thereover to the United States; and have the honor to request that you submit the same to the Legislature of your state at the earliest possible date, and use your good offices in securing early action thereon.

Very Respectfully,

Newton D. Baker
Secretary of War

APPENDIX D

The Senate and House of Representatives of the State of Delaware then met in General Assembly and granted to the United States, jurisdiction over the said lands. The Act granting the consent for use as a site for fortification read: (quoted letter)

AN ACT GRANTING THE CONSENT OF THE GENERAL ASSEMBLY OF THE STATE OF DELAWARE TO THE ACQUISITION BY THE UNITED STATES OF LANDS AT THE MOUTH OF THE MISPILLION RIVER IN CEDAR CREEK HUNDRED, SUSSEX COUNTY

Be it enacted by the Senate and House of Representatives of the State of Delaware in General Assembly met:

Section 1. That the consent of the Legislature of Delaware be and the same is hereby given, pursuant to the seventeenth clause of the eighth section of the first Article of the Constitution of the United States, to the purchase by the United States of one hundred fifty-one (151) acres and twenty (20) square perches of land in the vicinity of the mouth of the Mispillion River in Cedar Creek Hundred, Sussex County, for use as a site for fortifications, and to the requisition by purchase or proceedings in condemnation of such additional land adjacent thereto, not to exceed a total additional area of two hundred (200) acres, as may be required by the Federal government for the said purposes.

Section 2. Jurisdiction over the said lands, when the title thereto shall have been acquired, is hereby granted and ceded to the United States, *Provided,* that the sovereignty and jurisdiction of this state shall extend over the said lands so far as that all civil process as may issue under the authority of this State against any person or persons charged with crimes or other offenses committed without such lands may be executed thereon in the same way and manner as if this consent had not been given.

APPENDIX E

DETAILED ESTIMATES
COST OF DELIVERING GRAVEL
MISPILLION BATTERIES

ALL WATER DELIVERY

```
6 barges at $25 per day............  $150.00
1 tug at $200 per day..............   200.00
1 tug at $75 per day...............    75.00
             Total per day.........  $425.00

6 days at $425.......................$2,550.00
```

```
1500 tons - $2,550...............................  $1.66 per ton
Add for lost time due to weather.................    .55 per ton
                  Towing in river per ton......   $2.21
```

UNLOADING PLANT:

```
Wharf and derrick unloader.........$4,000.00
6500 feet track....................  7,500.00
4000 ties..........................  2,400.00
1 locomotive.......................  5,000.00
10 dump and 10 flat cars...........  6,000.00
Labor..............................  2,000.00
             Total.....$26,900.00
```

```
Charge off against 75,000 tons for unloading
plant.............................................     .36 per ton
Strengthening bins and trestles - $4,500
against 40,000 tons of sand and gravel........        .11 per ton
Unloading and operating siding..................      .30 per ton
             Total, delivery, per ton......        $2.98
Gravel, alongside dredge........................       .75
        Total cost of gravel delivered, per ton..  $3.73
        Total cost per yard, at 1.485 tons per yd. $5.54
```

> NOTE:- Estimate of 2.21 per ton for towing is $0.30 less than
> gravel company's estimate, without allowance for lost time.

RAILROAD SIDING — MILFORD TO CEDAR BEACH.

```
Net cost of siding for one year - Pennsylvania R.R. estimate.. $75,000
2 Locomotives..................................................  10,000
Sidings and switches at site...................................   6,000
                  Total................$91,000
```

```
Charge against 75,000 tons construction
materials and supplies, per ton...............  $1.21
Operating expenses, per ton...................    .15
Strengthening sand and gravel bins and trestles
$4,500 against 40,000 tons, per ton...........    .11
        Total cost delivery per ton...........  $1.47
Gravel f.o.b. Milford, per ton................   1.80
        Total cost gravel delivered per ton...  $3.27
        Total cost of gravel delivered per yard..  $4.85
```

DELIVERY BY RAILROAD SIDING AND MISPILLION CREEK.

```
Siding (Pennsylvania Railroad Co's estimate).................. $17,000
Switching engine..............................................   5,000
Trestle.......................................................   4,000 $26,000
```

```
Floating Plant:
6 barges at $250 per month each, 6 mos...................... $ 9,000
2 towing launches at $30 per day...........................   8,700 $17,700
```

```
Unloading Plant:
Wharf and unloader......................................... $ 4,000
Track......................................................   7,500
4,000 ties.................................................   2,400
Locomotives................................................   5,000
Cars.......................................................   6,000
Labor......................................................   2,000 $26,900
                  TOTAL...................... $69,900
```

150

REVISED ESTIMATE
FOR CONSTRUCTION OF BATTERIES
FOR 12" LONG RANGE GUNS NEAR MISPILLION RIVER, DELAWARE.

Quarters, kitchen, mess rooms, toilets, etc., for 100 men (white and colored)	$ 8,166
Field Office Building	1,370
Storehouse	517
Blacksmith Shop	659
Oil House	117
Sewer to Cedar Creek	1,860
Furniture, bedding, dishes, etc.	1,500
2 Boiler feed pumps	156
1 Water Tank, 10,000 gallons	1,200
1 Tank Pump (steam)	209
Miscellaneous Pipe and Fittings	4,500
2 Derricks, Hoists and miscellaneous plant not included in above	5,000
Auto delivery wagon	600
Two auto trucks (3 tons each) $7,000, operation $4,000	11,000
Miscellaneous tools and equipment	10,000
Excavation, 10,300 cu. yds. at 75¢	7,850
Extra work on account of subaqueous foundations for 4 gun platforms	5,000
Concrete in place, 25,480 cu. yds. at $14.627	372,696
Rehandling 30% gravel, sand and cement	6,000
Waterproofing, 8,780 sq. yds. at $2.00	17,560
Plumbing and drainage of batteries to sewer	4,700
Electric lighting, complete, including underground conduits	6,000
Trolley system in batteries	3,000
Steel doors, windows, shutters and miscellaneous fixtures throughout batteries, 15 tons in place at $300 per ton	4,500
Stairways and miscellaneous fixtures throughout batteries, 13 tons cast iron, in place at $200	2,600
Installation 25 k.w. gas motor sets, not including cost of sets	2,000
Painting, miscellaneous	5,000
Sand and earth cover for batteries, 60,000 cu. yds. at $1.50	90,000
Permanent road, walks, gutters, etc.	10,000
Removing construction plant, clearing ground, grading, etc.	10,000
Total	$589,447
Overhead and contingent expenses, etc. (10% of above)	58,945
Total	$648,392

INCLOSURE TO 3rd IND. - 20156/167

APPENDIX F

MB:JWC

October 24, 1917.

From: The District Engineer,
        U. S. Engineer Office,
        Wilmington, Del.

To: The Chief of Engineers,
        U. S. Army,
        Washington, D. C.

Subject: Shipment of armament for Fort Saulsbury, Del.

1. Construction work at Fort Saulsbury is in such shape that the mounting of one gun can be commenced about December 1, and of the second gun about two weeks thereafter. The two remaining guns can probably not be mounted until sometime in February, depending upon weather conditions this winter.

2. The guns and armament will have to be brought to the site on light draught barges of about 350 tons capacity. The conditions will be unfavorable for handling these barges in the Delaware Bay after about the 1st of December, and it is therefore recommended that arrangements be made to ship all, or such parts of guns and mountings as may be available, as early as practicable, in order that they may be shipped to the site while weather conditions are suitable.

3. Shipment should be made to Philadelphia, Pa., where the material can be loaded on barges. There are no facilities for unloading this material from cars and loading on barges at Wilmington.

Major, Corps of Engineers.

20156/187   1st Ind.   JWC/

Office, Chief of Engineers, Oct. 30, 1917 - TO THE CHIEF OF ORDNANCE.

Information is requested as to the approximate time when the armament for Fort Saulsbury (4 12-inch) will be ready for shipment.

Major General, Chief of Engineers.

Armament Shipment dates from the District Engineer in Wilmington, DE, to Chief of Engineers in Washington, D.C.

ILLUSTRATIONS

On the cover is a photograph taken at Fort Saulsbury about 1919 by Mrs. Augusta Wigley.

SOURCES

FORT SAULSBURY

A Mighty Fort Called Miles
C.W. Warrington, 1972

Big Thursday
By Anne Z. Sparklin
Dorrance and Co.
Philadelphia, PA, 1966

Stuart L. Butler
Navy and Old Army Branch
National Archives, Washington, D.C.

The Chronicle Newspaper, Milford, DE

Delaware Place Names
United States Department of the Interior Geological Survey
L.W. Heck, A.J. Wraight, D.J Orth, J.R. Carter,
L.G. Van Winkle, and J. Hazen

Every Evening Newspaper, Wilmington, DE 1917

Fort Record Books
Fort Du Pont, Delaware, 1901-1943
Fort Du Pont, Delaware, 1900-1915

Harpers School Geography
Ritter and Humboldt, 1880
New York, Harper and Brothers

History of Delaware
J. Thomas Scharf
L.J. Richards and Co., Philadelphia, PA 1888

History of the State of Delaware
By Henry C. Conrad
Wilmington, DE, 1908

Journal Every Evening Newspaper, Wilmington, DE 1940

The Mother Earth News
Hendersonville, NC, 1983

Order of Battle of the United States Land Forces in the World War
Zone of the Interior
Volume Three, Part I
U.S. Government Printing Office, Washington, D.C., 1916

The Poetical and Prose Writings of John Lofland: The Milford Bard
Published by John Murphy and Co.
Wilmington, DE—J.T. Heard, 1853

Records of the Office of the Chief of Engineers
National Archives, Washington, D.C.

Records of the United States Army Commands
(Army Posts) RG 98

Shoreline Erosion Control
U.S. Army Corps of Engineers
Philadelphia District, 1980

United States Military Reservations
National Cemeteries and Military Parks
U.S. Government Printing Office, Washington D.C., 1916

War Department Military Reservations
U.S. Government Printing Office, Washington, D.C., 1937

Water Analysis Laboratories
St. Paul, MN, 1983
For Sears, Roebuck and Company
Sears Tower, Chicago, IL

Mrs. Augusta Wigley
Slaughter Beach and Fort Saulsbury photographs

SOURCES

A MIGHTY FORT CALLED MILES

A History of the United States
John Frost, 1843
Thomas, Cowperthwait & Co., Philadelphia

A History of the United States of America
Rev. Charles A. Goodrich, 1824
Barber & Robinson, Hartford

The Amazing Mrs. Bonaparte
Harnett T. Kane, 1963
Garden City, New York

The American Conflict
A History of the Great Rebellion
Horace Greeley, 1866
O.D. Case & Co., Hartford

The Archeolog Vol. XV, No. 1
H.G. Omwake, T.D. Stewart, M.C. Blaker, and J. Wittholf, 1963
Sussex Society of Archeology and History

Buffalo Bill Historical Center
Cody Wyoming

Custer Battlefield
Robert M. Utley
National Park Service, U. S. Department of the Interior
Washington, D.C., 1969

The Delaware Citizen
Cy Liberman and James M. Rosbrow, 1952
Life Insurance Company of North America
Wilmington, DE

Delaware Conservationist
Winter Issue, 1968

Delaware Place Names
    L.G. Van Winkle, and J. Hazen
    L.J. Richards and Co., Philadelphia, PA 1888
    L.W. Heck, A.J. Wraight, D.J Orth, J.R. Carter,

Delaware State Museum
    Dover, DE

Delaware: A History of the First State
    Edited by H. Clay Reed, 1947, New York
    Lewes Historical Publishing Co.

The Delmarva Peninsula
    Hearn Oil Co., 1926

Dictionary of American History
    James Truslow Adams
    Editor-in-Chief, 1936-1949
    Charles Scribner's Sons, NY

The Encyclopedia Britannica
    William Benton, Publisher

Essentials in American History
    Albert B. Hart, LL.D., 1905
    American Book Company, NY

Fort Delaware
    W. Emerson Wilson, 1957
    University of Delaware Press

General Services Administration
    National Archives
    Washington, D.C.

Geography of Delaware
    Harper and Brothers, 1876, NY

History of Delaware
    J. Thomas Scharf
    Philadelphia, 1888. L.J. Richards, Publisher

History of Lewes, Delaware
Virginia Cullen, 1956
Colonel David Hall Chapter, Daughters of the American Revolution
Lewes, DE

Indians of Delaware
C.A. Weslanger, 1953
University of Delaware Press

National Audubon Society Magazine
May/June, 1967

The Nation's National Guard
National Guard Association of the United States
Washington, D.C., 1954

Rules and Regulations
State Park Commission of Delaware
June, 1968

Selected articles from the *Wilmington Evening Journal* and *Journal-Every Evening*

State Indian Museum
Sacramento, CA

Stories and Legends of the Delaware Capes
William P. Frank
Miles L. Frederick, Publisher, Wilmington, DE
United States Department of the Interior Geological Survey

West Point Museum, United States Military Academy
West Point, NY

The World Book Encyclopedia
Quarrie Corporation, 1947

World War II Collector's Shop and Museum (Argo Corner)
Milford, DE

Zwaanendael Museum
Lewes, DE